To Will God's Will

Books by Ben Campbell Johnson
Published by The Westminster Press

To Will God's Will: Beginning the Journey

To Pray God's Will: Continuing the Journey

Rethinking Evangelism: A Theological Approach

To Will God's Will

Beginning the Journey

Ben Campbell Johnson

The Westminster Press
Philadelphia

Book design by Gene Harris

First edition

Published by The Westminster Press®

Louisville, Kentucky 40202

PRINTED IN THE UNITED STATES OF AMERICA

9 8 7 6 5

Library of Congress Cataloging-in-Publication Data

Johnson, Ben Campbell.
  To will God's will.

  1. Spiritual life—Presbyterian authors.
I. Title.
BV4501.2.J539 1987   248   87-14271
ISBN 0-664-24086-0 (pbk.)

Contents

Preface

For a long time I have been concerned about the will of God—how to find it and fulfill it—in my life. This concern has taken me on a search for myself, for my soul. On this inward journey I have made some discoveries that I believe have helped me. I would like to share them with you because I believe they will also have meaning for you.

I am writing to you as a companion on the journey, not as a tour guide bored with describing the same scenes repeatedly. As your companion I will at times look ahead but then come back and stand by your side; and when I describe the terrain over which we travel, I will again be a learner with you.

I am writing to Christians from a Christian perspective. I have made no effort to justify the faith to a rationalist thinker. I assume that you believe in God, that you see in Christ a hope for your life. I do not assume that you believe profoundly or that you have a theological education. You can benefit from what I have to say if you simply wish to know God better.

In this book I will develop a frame of reference, a way of looking at life. This perspective will include notions about how your natural life becomes the arena for the activity of God. The perspective, the exercises, and the suggestions intend to help you notice God's presence and be receptive to it. The companion volume, *To Pray God's Will: Continuing the Journey,* will focus on the unconscious and its role in spirituality, plus an emphasis on the disciplines of contemplation and silence.

You may use one or both of these volumes in various ways: (1) as a personal guide for your own faith journey; (2) as the text for a small group or a Sunday school class, or (3) as the basis for a special emphasis on prayer or Christian spirituality.

To understand the perspective from which I am writing, you need to know that I had a dramatic conversion experience nearly forty years ago. Ever since that day I have been a serious Christian, not always obedient but always deeply concerned about God in my life. Yet my quest led to a strange and bewildering experience. I discovered two sides to my life—a religious side and a secular side. This division resulted in a split between faith and life. I have struggled over the years to discover faith in life and to experience life saturated with faith.

Getting these two aspects of life together has taken me more than half my Christian life. This struggle has influenced the way I have begun this journey with you. In this search for wholeness I offer myself to you as a guide.

As your companion/guide I will describe an important notion that shapes the spiritual life. In Appendix A I will outline a way for you to appropriate that idea. To have sophisticated concepts about your relation with God has little meaning until you submit yourself to experience the reality of God.

Appendix B also contains an extensive section on journal keeping. I hope you will document your experiences in a permanent record. I promise that this effort will be rewarded handsomely.

I anticipate an exciting journey with you.

The affirmation of Albert Schweitzer in the closing lines of his famous study, *The Quest of the Historical Jesus,* is appropriate for spiritual journeyers:

> He comes to us as one unknown, without a name, as of old, by the lakeside, He came to those men who knew him not. He speaks to us the same word: "Follow thou me!" And sets us to the tasks which he has to fulfill for our time. He commands. And to those who obey him, whether they be wise or simple, He will reveal himself in the toils, the conflicts, the sufferings which they shall pass through in his fellowship, and, as an ineffable mystery, they will learn in their own experience who he is.[1]

My appreciation goes to my wife, Nan, who helped immeasurably with the preparation of this manuscript, and to my friends Dr. Douglas Hix and Dean Oscar Hussel, who aided with their criticism and suggestions.

New Year's, 1987

1

The Spiritual Journey

***What is life but a journey
from birth to God?***

If I am to be your guide, we must begin at the beginning, the beginning of your life, of your being. To arrive at this starting point requires more than a mere statement, "Once upon a time you were born!" Make an effort to "feel" what it is like to be, to come into being. Can you imagine what it is like to begin to be? Perhaps this meditation will be of more help to you than a discourse.

I am.
There was a time when I was not.
There will come a time when I am no longer.
But, now, I am.
I am alive!
Life is creation's gift, unsought and unexpected. Suddenly, out of nowhere, I appeared, with no excuse to boast or reason to feel shame.
The mystery of being expressed itself in that creative moment when the egg and sperm met in the dark cavern of my mother's womb. The long night began, a time of waiting without awareness until the day dawned. This dark night bespeaks the mystery that from the be-

ginning surrounds life, a mystery that like a cloud shadows me throughout life.

As a new life I waited to express myself, to collect my experiences of being, to ask my questions, to wonder at the reason for my entry on the stage of this human drama.

From the first moment of life I, a unique expression of a Creator, carried within myself a mystery, the mystery of my own reason for being.

Without awareness I began preparation for my entry into the human family. At the time appointed I came forth to start my journey through life.

So tiny, so fragile, so utterly dependent, and only with a frown or a cry or perhaps a clutched hand could I signal pain or discontent. And the response that I received told me about the safety or threat of my new world.

In those early days when a cry or whimper was my only form of speech, that blank era before things had names, before objects had connection, I discovered my mother's face and began to trust its regular appearance. Her face provided a constant in the new world of uncertainty. Like a beacon her face appeared and disappeared, assuring me of one trustworthy object. With this assurance I embarked on the voyage.

The early years of life may be compared to waking up and finding yourself a stowaway on board a ship. It's too late to get off. You are already on a voyage without knowing how you got there, what you are doing, or where you are going.

From the very beginning of the journey, you experience the paradox of your life. You feel that something within you knows who you are, why you are here, and where you are going, but this knowledge is submerged, hidden. Because you cannot perceive it directly, you ask about it, seeking the answer in everything you do.

Until you consciously ask the question, the hunger for meaning remains a vague, unidentified feeling, more like an ache or a void than a well-formed question. But with the acquisition of words, plus a sense of time—such as yesterday and tomorrow—you ask the question for yourself, "Where did I come from?" This question is itself an important signpost; it indicates an awareness that you realize you have not always been.

When you first ask the question of origin, you mean, "Where did I come from physically?" Later you ask this question with respect to time. "Where was I before I got here?" Do you remember how difficult it was trying to imagine a time when you were not? How threatening, too! Later on, you ask the question meaning, "Where did I come from socially? What are my roots?"

Somewhat later in your life you ask still another question, "Who am I?" You were given parents. A name. A place in a family. An address. You assume this is your identity. In your adolescent years the question of "Who am I?" becomes so strong that you cannot avoid asking it in a thousand different ways. From the answers given you by parents, peers, and mentors you shape a fragile identity.

After you tentatively resolve this major crisis, you begin to say "I" with a new sense of power and integrity. Yet the question of identity persists at every stage of life, possibly never exhausted or answered fully until the journey's end.

A third question plagues the adolescent, often persisting into maturity: "What's wrong with me?" All persons, when they face their deepest feelings, have an uneasiness, an awareness that they are not what they were created to be. The feeling of being alienated from oneself intensifies the search for identity.

You are. You know that you are. You have asked the

questions of origin, identity, and alienation. In late adolescence or early adulthood, you ask yet another crucial question, "Why am I here?" This question, unimaginable to a child and only anticipated by most adolescents, is asked with total seriousness when you face the choices of a mate, a vocation, and parenthood. These choices provide the structure for your life.

Like the question of identity, the inquiry into purpose never ends. A move to a new city, job dissatisfaction, a persistent feeling of emptiness, the last child leaving home, retirement—all these experiences tamper with our sense of purpose and repeatedly force the questions, "Why am I here? What is the purpose of my life?"

The final question regards destiny. "Where am I going?" At some level this question bespeaks an anxiety about life goals—whether you'll reach them and if they're worth reaching. But at another level this question, either consciously or unconsciously, points toward death. "Where am I going when my life is finished?" you ask.

These fundamental questions about existence shape our interpretations of our life experiences. I recall my experience of these questions. The first came around age seven. I asked my mother, "Where did I come from?" She answered directly but without too much detail. Behind the question was an awareness that I had not always been, an idea that staggered me.

My question of identity began to emerge in the sixth grade. I had noticed Jane, a girl in my class. When she smiled at me, I felt something inside. I didn't know what to call this sensation, but it felt good, and I responded to her. I had fantasies about standing close to her, even touching her. These feelings and fantasies caused me to wonder who I was in relation to her.

After my introduction to my male identity by my response to Jane, I began trying out different forms of that identity. I spent hours in front of the mirror making sure my hair and clothes looked just right while I tried to avoid noticing the blemishes that were all too obvious.

The question of my identity, awakened with the birth of my sexuality, did not rest with these early answers. I knew that a part of who I was came from my family. I also assumed that my clothes, my friends, the car the family drove, and where we lived all contributed to my sense of who I was.

I suppose that before the age of twelve I had a vague sense of "wrongness," but I had no name to give it. At twelve an incident happened that I recall vividly. Billy Vaughan, my next-door neighbor, was watching me pull nut grass from my mother's rose bed. In a burst of rage at the hopelessness of the task and the demand that I do a job I had not the slightest interest in doing, I swore. I gave a few concise descriptions of that nut grass and what I hoped would happen to it! Billy laughed at me. I thought, "If you think that was funny, listen to what else I can say!" The consequent daring stream of profanity marked my first step over the line to do what was known, willful wrong. While I enjoyed the pleasure of being noticed by my friend, that sense of power it brought me soon faded into fear and mistrust. "What if Billy tells his mother, and what if she tells my mother?" I quickly began to experience the pain of guilt before I knew what name to give it.

Actually, I had become aware of the question of my destiny before I had a sense of personal guilt. The question of my future confronted me at age nine when I walked alone across the highway at my Uncle John's, near the very spot where my great-grandfather had been hit by an automobile and fatally injured. Suddenly death became very personal. As I walked across that road, the question impacted itself on me: "What will happen to *me* when I die?"

I could not deal with it. Though the weather was sultry, I shivered as the chill awareness of my own death paralyzed my mind. Often, after that marker day, the reality of my death confronted me. Because I did not then have a religious background, I had no notion of a loving God who would be with me even in death. My only way of coping with this disturbing reality was to put off thinking about it until I grew older; but try as I might, I could not escape the continuing awareness that I am dependent on another for my life and that one day life as I now know it will end.

The awareness of my life's finiteness has, I suspect, fueled the intensity with which I have asked, "Why am I here?" I did not ask this question seriously until the third decade of my life. Toward the end of that decade I began to fear that I might live my whole life for naught. "What if I should come to the end of life, look back, and discover that I have spent my time to no avail?" Since then I have continued to grapple earnestly with the meaning of my life. I still do.

How have these questions presented themselves to you? How have you begun to answer them? You may think that you have ignored these questions, and consciously you may have, but in some way they have always been present to your life experience. Through your choices and interpretations of your life experiences you have been answering these questions each day of your life. In answering these human questions, in whatever way you have, you still leave untouched the larger question: "What is my life?"

The strange, mysterious beginning, this fragile, impressionable character on which early conditioning leaves such deep and permanent marks, causes me to wonder, "What is my life? How am I to understand it?

What is the metaphor that best describes it? What is the paradigm that captures the meaning of my experience of being?"

Persons arrive at contrasting conclusions. They answer this ultimate human question in the values they adopt, in the goals they seek, and in the way they structure their lives. By these criteria they say:

"Life is a party, a good time—grab with all the gusto you can."

"Life is a test, an endurance test, in which I pit myself against the calamities, hardships, and unexpected pain of human existence."

"Life is like a game—a game in which persons seek to win all the money and honor and power they can."

"Life is a drama. We are actors, all playing our parts. We mask our true identity in the pretense of our roles."

"Life is nothing, a zero, boring with its repetition, going nowhere."

"Life is waiting—waiting for the fulfillment and meaning that never come."

If you were to select a symbol for the meaning of your life, what would it be today? If you think about your life, a being that has come on the stage of history, a life that hungers for meaning and asks the most basic questions imaginable and answers these questions with concrete decisions, what symbol would you adopt? What image expresses your life?

I am painfully aware that some persons think of their life as a game, a part, a drama, or a zero, but all these seem inadequate to express the meaning of my life. They lack depth. I do not sense meaning flowing from these metaphors. There is a metaphor, however, that I believe captures the meaning of my life, and that is the *journey.*

Comparing life to a journey does not come with any particular newness or surprise. Writers through the centuries have used this metaphor. The Bible traces the history of Israel from Egypt to the Promised Land; the Israelites found the identity and meaning of their nation's life on their journey. Chaucer, in *The Canterbury Tales,* organizes his collection of stories in a journey motif. Dante, in *The Divine Comedy,* uses the journey motif to describe the descent and ascent of the soul. The myths of all cultures contain stories of their heroes' departure, victory over the enemy, and return.

Because of its richness and its power to suggest the meaning of life, I like the image of the journey. Life is a journey from birth to death and beyond. Change is implicit in a journey. Journey suggests movement and individual participation.

The journey metaphor has special meaning for me because in my youthful idealism I had an image of an achievement, a place to stand, a destination, a place of arrival—a paradise, if you will—where all our tensions are relieved, our relationships straightened out, and our problems solved. I sought through various means to return to this Eden of perfection. "Surely," I thought, "if I discipline myself, I can get there." Discipline failed. I reasoned further, "Possibly the way to this peace and unity comes from knowledge." Knowledge failed. My last means was experience. "If I can receive some overwhelming experience, a peak moment of being, I will attain this personal and spiritual utopia." Experience failed.

All these means failed to lead me to utopia because it is literally "no place." Utopia, *ou topos,* means *no place.* There is nowhere to retreat where all questions are answered, all problems solved, and life is perfect. With this disillusionment I began to realize that life is a journey. It is a series of changes and transitions. There is no utopia, no stationary place, because life is a process. The secret of life lies in being open to its movement, responsive to its demands. In this vision of life as a journey, peace, unity, and wholeness come from a maturity that accepts incompleteness and ambiguity. The journey metaphor aptly describes my life because it implies that life is a process of unfolding, of discovery, of change, with change being the only constant.

The journey metaphor makes room for failure. Journeys are seldom made without incident, occurrences that redirect our lives:

Detours
Dead-end streets
Accidents
Weariness
Traffic jams
Getting lost

Journeys include these interruptions, and so does life. Hasn't your life encountered some of these obstacles?

How does the notion of "journey" speak to you? Does it gather up your life experience with meaning? Are there aspects of this metaphor that pinpoint your life's adventure?

At the beginning of our pilgrimage into the spiritual journey I would like you to begin gathering together the vignettes of your life in this journey metaphor. The spiritual journey begins with the natural journey. I have said nothing yet about the spiritual dimension of this journey you are making; that adventure still lies before us.

Please turn to Exercise 1 in Appendix B, "How Life Is like a Journey," for help in thinking about your life as a spiritual journey. If you have not already done so, please read Appendix A, "Journaling," and begin now to keep your own spiritual journal.

2

The Substance
of the Journey

*A personal myth is the story
we tell ourselves about the things
that have happened
to us on the journey.*

The journey metaphor provides a sufficiently large picture to include the varied aspects of our lives. The journey has a beginning, an ending, and all the substance lying between those all-important markers. Consider the question of the substance, the "stuff" that lies between the beginning and end of your life and how it relates to your journey.

As a seminary professor, I frequently meet with students who need guidance on their spiritual journey. One young man had come to seminary with the notion that God had chosen him to be a minister, but the wear and tear of studies linked with the neglect of disciplines that had enriched his life in the past had created a dry, empty feeling about his life. After laying out his concern, he asked, "What am I going to do to recover my sense of direction?"

"If you intend to deal constructively with the problem," I began, "you must begin with your history, the story of your life. To discern your story, it is necessary for you to recognize the important events in your life, the interpretation you have given them, and how you have connected them into a narrative."

As I seek to guide you on your journey, I give you the same advice. Discover the important events in your life and the story you are telling about those events. "Why," you may ask, "are you thrusting me back into my past? What do all those past experiences have to do with a 'spiritual journey'?"

Everything. The spiritual journey must never be thought of as a trek separate from real-life experience. The spiritual journey is the story of our lives in relation to God, but that relationship is another issue that we will face later on.

Your question about the past and its relation to your spiritual journey invites more explanation. Your life journey has five components: *events, perception, interpretation,. connection,* and *narrative.* By events I mean occurrences, happenings, encounters with persons, ideas, memories, or dreams for your life. "Event" points to the raw data of personal experience, the stuff from which you construct the meaning of your life.

What do you consider to be the "stuff" of your life? I would answer that question first by stating that a dozen or so significant events have been the basic material of my life. To begin with, "I was born." That statement contains the foundation for anything else that I can say. "I was born in the country" amplifies the statement about my birth and points to the setting of my early years. As I continue to reflect on my life, I can add one significant event after another until I come to the most recent, "called to teach at Columbia Theological Seminary."

How do these events relate to my journey? These occurrences in my life form the building blocks out of which my life journey is constructed. If you are to understand your journey, you must be willing to look at your history, the experiences you have had that form you as a person.

Each of us has had numerous experiences. Many of these occurred without any self-awareness on our part, and at the moment they seemed to have no significant role in our lives. The events to which I am referring are those you perceived; that is, you were aware that something was happening to you at a certain time.

But the journey is more than events and perceptions; it includes the interpretation of those formative events of your life. Events do not automatically come to you with an interpretation. You provide the interpretation yourself. Suppose that you are a teenage boy quite uncertain of your male identity. You call a young lady in your junior class to whom you have felt some attraction. Hearing your invitation to go out with you on a date, she responds, "Sorry, I can't make it Friday night." The only meaning present in the words is an apology that she cannot see you on one particular evening. But how easy it is for a young man to say, "I'm unattractive. She doesn't like me." Or, "Girls just don't care for me." The boy interprets the event for himself. In a similar way each of us has interpreted the events of our lives.

Once an event has been interpreted, its meaning must be woven into the fabric created by the interpretations of other occurrences. Each new interpretation is like a patch that is sewn into the quilt of meaning we are creating. Think again about the teenage boy calling a girl for a date. Assume for a moment that he has a good sense of selfhood; he likes himself and feels comfortable with girls. When he receives a rejection from one girl, he has no need to interpret this onetime rejection as proving that he is not attractive. Rather, he accepts the fact that she is probably already committed and he can try again on another day. The rejection for him receives no greater meaning than it deserves.

This act of weaving the meaning of an event into the fabric of our life is the creation of a narrative. Each of us is telling a story that is constructed from the interpretation of the occurrences of our lives. In each of the references of the boy calling a classmate for a date, a story is being created by what he tells himself about himself and his world. But the experience with the girl is only one example of hundreds of interpretations that blend together to form his life's story.

The story that we tell ourselves and that is constructed from the events of our lives is our perceived meaning. Our story is who we are. Or, we are our story!

The narrative of each of our life journeys answers the primal questions: Where did I come from? What am I doing here? What is wrong with me? What is the purpose of my life? Where am I going? What happens to me when I die? The narrative of each one's journey is a personalized construction of life's meaning. Humans have always asked these questions, and their answers woven together constitute the meaning of their lives.

Real-life events—the places we go, the people we meet, the jobs we hold, the successes and failures we experience, our dreams and hopes—provide the substance of the journey. They are the landscape of our journey. We have all experienced these happenings and shaped such experiences into a narrative—a story of our lives. If you wish to know who you are, discover your life story. This narrative of the happenings of your life is your identity.

Because this concept is crucial for the developing of your spiritual journey, I want you to look more deeply into the process of translating events into a narrative. An analogy may be helpful. Inside you is a camera, a tape recorder, a translator, an editor, and a narrator. These characters take charge of translating events into a story.

The camera functions as your eyes, which perceive the events. Your ears are like microphones attached to a high-fidelity recorder. In the deep underside of your being, a translator interprets the meaning of these sights and sounds. The translator always interprets according to the norms and values of the society around you unless a drastic intervention alters this perspective. Another function of the translator is that of editing. Because of the perceptual system, certain occurrences are not perceived, while others that contradict the desires and norms of the person are blocked out.

As the translator attaches a meaning to the event, the narrator connects the meaning given the event to the ongoing story of your life. Your life-meaning unfolds with the connecting of each bit of interpretation. (Note that these are functions of the mind and are thus not totally separate from each other. The mind functions with all these different capacities.) Let me illustrate how this operates. When I was nine years old, my parents moved from the country to Elba, Alabama, a small town about six miles from my birthplace. I recall looking into the face of my third-grade teacher and saying, "I will miss you and all my friends." She encouraged me. "But you will be making many new friends, and you'll do well in school!" This encounter signaled the transition from my being a country boy to a town boy.

As I stood there talking with Miss Claudia, a marker event of my life was occurring. My eyes saw her, the room, and the woods behind the school. Those pictures are still there in my memory. My ears heard and my recorder retained the words she uttered. My translator took those sights and sounds and ascribed meaning to them. The translator first said, "You are experiencing a change in houses, in schools, in teachers and friends. This will be just fine for you." Since I was anxious about being "a little country boy," these words quelled my fears. My narrator received these words of encouragement and gave me a positive picture of the move to town. I suppose that is about all that happened on the conscious level, but there was more meaning in that event than a nine-year-old could abstract.

Each time I recall that event, I see a deeper significance. It marked a move away from my roots, but I took with me the meaning of being a rural child during the Depression. From those roots I draw an understanding of the rural mentality. The experience of being poor probably still drives me to work too much and to "save for a rainy day."

This perceiving, recording, translating, filing process operates on two levels: the conscious level, of course, and a deeper level, distant to us and unreachable by our will. There perceptions are being stored in memory, where they continue their influence on our unsuspecting consciousness. Once experienced, a meaningful event, whether positive or negative in its impact, is always present in our deeper self, shaping and directing us.

The interpreter within us constantly looks for meaning. This functionary keeps asking, "What does this mean? How does this relate to the whole of life?" Each event of our life, particularly events that mark important transitions, receives an ascription of meaning. Each time we reflect on that event, we perceive deeper and broader implications of it for our lives. That event of moving to town meant one thing in 1941, but each time I have recalled it since that year, its significance has been expanded.

Not all events are as easily assimilated as a move from the country to town. We face a different set of problems when events occur to which we cannot easily ascribe a meaning. These events are hard; they resist our penetration. They don't make sense because they contradict the story we have been telling. They often contradict it so completely that we wonder if our life does in fact have meaning, if there is a future worth having. When I was thirteen, my family moved from Elba to Enterprise, Alabama. I was not as deeply affected by this move, but I was stunned by an event that happened in this new life setting. For three years I had had a small dog named Chubby. Chubby was part cocker spaniel and part Boston bull, but her most important characteristic was her complete love and devotion to me. She went everywhere with me and especially loved to ride in the basket of my bike. When she faced into the wind, her long ears resembled wings as they were supported by the rush of air.

One day I came home to discover that Chubby was gone. My dad had given her away. Crushed, I fled to my room and cried and cried.

"Why?" I kept asking my mother between sobs.

"Because she is always going into heat, and we don't have anywhere to keep her."

That did not resolve my pain. All my questioning of Dad and my pleading with him to retrieve Chubby were to no avail. Chubby was gone.

About ten days later I came home from school to find Chubby waiting for me. Had Dad changed his mind? No. Chubby had missed me too. She had run away from her new owner and found her way back to me. I was ecstatic.

But when Dad came home that evening, he insisted that Chubby go back to her new owner. Not even my tears could change the decision.

I recall the depth of pain because to me Dad's decision carried the finality of death. I lamented that Chubby would never come home; I would never see her; she was gone forever. These feelings of grief and helplessness tormented me for weeks.

At this point the interpreter in my head could not make sense of my loss. Why had my dad made this decision? What did this mean for my future? For a few months I could not imagine a future at all, much less a positive one. Such a traumatic event may remain undigested in the midst of a life story, waiting to be revisited, reconciled, and made a part of one's ongoing personal narrative.

In addition to traumatic events, there are also occasions in which we experience peak moments, moments when we see more clearly who we are and the meaning of our lives. A conversation with a friend, a sunset, a moment of feeling loved, the joy of success, a worship service, a baby's first steps—any of these and a thousand other events may become bearers of a significant moment to us. These events come to us with a power that will not permit us to ignore them. They do not bypass the interpreter within us but seem to have a voice of their own. They speak to us: "This is who you are. This is what you are to do."

A friend of mine described such an experience: "On this particular Sunday morning in worship it seemed the words of the minister were directed especially to me. God spoke to me through them. At the close of the service he asked those who wished to respond to God to please stand. I stood. That day was a turning point, a marker event in my life."

Prior to that encounter she had had no definitive experience of God. During her first thirty years she had no religious training. She did not attend church or know anything about faith. From her midwestern home she traveled each summer to New Mexico. There she was exposed to the blaze of nature with a color and majesty that convinced her of the Divine. Her summers spent in the great Southwest, filled with visions of the majesty of mountains and blue sky, gave her a certain peace and confidence. But when she returned home, she lost the sense of God. She had no images, no religious symbols with which to interpret this experience and thus to weave it into the meaning of her life.

Between the ages of thirty and forty-five she affiliated with a Christian church in which she heard the message and appropriated the symbols. With these images she was able to name the Spirit of God who spoke through the minister and to label her encounter/response as a "conversion." With these symbols she could appropriate and nurture her life with God.

A conversion experience for many demonstrates this quality of life transformation. A person within the Christian community hears Christ in one of the thousand ways he speaks. This confrontation has an authority the subject cannot ignore. Because this event occurs in the context of the church, the subject has a set of symbols with which to ascribe a preliminary meaning to the event.

My life was changed by just such an encounter with Christ. I had been deeply affected by a friend who asked me, "If Christ returned, would you be on his side?" Though I answered in the negative, he told me of Christ's love for me. I attended church that evening in a different frame of mind. I listened to the minister. God, I believe, spoke to me. In that meeting my mind was shaken. I felt an ache, then an emptiness. Deep within I said, "Yes, God." Not at that moment, but an hour or so later, a divine awareness broke into my consciousness. God took hold of me. The events of this evening carried a power that convinced me I had met God. My translator did not interpret this event; it interpreted itself. The experience marked the end of one life and the beginning of another and opened a new world for me both spiritually and intellectually. It was a watershed event holding within it a clue to my future.

While that event did interpret itself to a degree, the full meaning of it has not been exhausted in more than thirty-five years. Each time I review my life, that day still stands out as one of its most important days, not because of some dramatic emotional experience but because it continues to give both rootage and direction to my life today.

In describing the substance of our lives I have stressed the events that occur, the awareness we have of those events, the interpretation we give them, and the manner in which we weave them into a narrative, the story of our lives. The combination of these little vignettes forms the master story of our lives.

Consider how important and powerful is the master story of your life. This story provides you with an identity. To discover who you are, look at your story. The story you tell is the embodiment of your self.

The master story creates a perspective on life. By perspective I mean a particular way of seeing life, other persons, God, and ourselves. This peculiar weaving together of events from a given perspective creates the fabric of our lives. Woven into that fabric are the symbols, values, and goals that have informed us.

Finally, our master story, by its implicit plot, hints at the aim of our lives. To make this affirmation implies a high level of congruence between who we are and how we perceive ourselves. Someone has said, "There is Something within each of us that knows who we are and what we are to do!" Even though we acknowledge that we are sinful and broken, there is still enough of God within us that we cannot suppress that which longs to actualize the purpose for which we were created. The more our actual lives are congruent with the intention within us, the more they exemplify the person we were created to be.

What is the story you have told about the events of your life? This story contains the meaning of your life at this present moment. My intention in setting forth the way we construct our narrative is to ask you to open up your story, to become aware of your narrative through an identification of the events that support it. The spiritual journey begins with our concrete life experience and the meaning we have ascribed to it. All spiritual transformation begins with this reality, the substance of our lives as we perceive it.

Many persons live their life stories without ever becoming aware of their drama. The curtain is pulled, one act ends and another begins without these persons' ever noting the change. To an onlooker it would appear that they live with no sense of participation in their destiny. Proceeding from one day to another, they live unconsciously, blind to the repetitions in their days and weeks, failing to discern any meaning in their choices, and taking little or no initiative in the shaping of their future.

If life is worth living, it is worth an examination. A citizen of Santa Maria, Italy, where Leonardo da Vinci was painting his famous *Last Supper,* wrote: "I watched Leonardo work from dawn to dusk without putting down his brush. Then he would pause and not put his brush to the canvas for days, but spend a few hours each day looking at it, examining and evaluating its figures." Living is a lot like painting in that we need to pause occasionally and view the picture we are creating with our lives.

To be sure, the thought of self-reflection produces anxiety in many persons. A friend recently said to me, "Don't ask me to look into my history. I'm not interested. The very thought of it terrifies me." The invitation to take a look at your story may release an unnamed fear that makes you want to slam the door on the past. I hope you will not yield to that fear. Resolve to risk as much as you can. You will know how much reflection you can handle. The past does not disappear just because you refuse to acknowledge it. The past invades every moment, coloring feelings, motivating decisions, and controlling behavior. We cannot run away from our history; it is us!

Can you identify the major events from which you have created your master story? You have lived this many years. You have experienced a number of life-shaping events. You have already constructed a narrative about these events and woven these small stories into a master story of your life. Here is a simple process for you to begin opening up your life story.

Begin with your earliest memory. Place yourself in the environment of your first years. Think of the house in which you lived, your family members, and your place in the family. Very slowly, quietly, reflectively let your life pass before you. Do not judge yourself; do not block out unpleasant memories; let your life happen before your eyes.

As you move through your life journey leading up to the present, note the signposts along the road. A signpost is a marker event, an event that indicates a transition. After you passed that point, your life took on a different meaning. Your life review should produce ten or twelve signposts or marker events. With just a word or a phrase, jot down the marker. These might read: Born in Atlanta, moved to Chicago, sister born, and so forth.

Following the procedure I have outlined for you, I discover these signposts:

1. Born in the country
2. A move to town
3. Growing up feeling anxious
4. Conversion to Christ
5. College and seminary
6. Starting the Lay Witness Mission

7. Graduate school and beginning the Institute of Church Renewal

8. Life breaking apart

9. New—all things new

10. Call—reconfirmed

11. A new future

These phrases include more than geographical moves and external events. They recall to me the texture of each aspect of the journey.

After you have written the list of your events, reflect on the space between each of them. What was happening to you during this time? Who were the important persons? What was your life like? After asking these questions, give each of these spaces a name that depicts the quality or meaning of your life in that period.

When you finish writing, read over the substance of your life as you perceive it today. Reading over these markers will help you feel a movement, a sense that the things that have happened to you are connected and have meaning. You will discover a source of strength for your life. As you begin to identify the flow of your life, you can project the direction of your life into the future. Awareness of the varied stories we live out and the persons we are requires us to accept the dark, fearful experiences of our past and to interpret these hidden parts of our lives. This enables us to weave the negative into our story.

In his poetic way of expressing truth, Frederick Buechner, in *The Sacred Journey*, describes the substance of our lives as the events that have happened to us and suggests that these are God's ways of working with us:

> The question is not whether the things that happen to you are chance things or God's things because, of course, they are both at once. There is no chance thing

through which God cannot speak—even the walk from the house to the garage that you have walked ten thousand times before, even the moments when you cannot believe there is a God who speaks at all anywhere. He speaks, I believe, and the words he speaks are incarnate in the flesh and blood of our selves and of our own footsore and sacred journeys. We cannot live our lives constantly looking back, listening back, lest we be turned to pillars of longing and regret, but to live without listening at all is to live deaf to the fullness of the music.[1]

For guidance in looking more deeply into your spiritual journey see Exercise 2, "The Chapters of Your Life," in Appendix B.

3

The Spiritual Depth
of the Journey

*Our foundational beliefs
provide the lenses through which
we view the pathway to God.*

The young woman sitting next to me on the flight from New York to Atlanta seemed curious about the book I was reading, *You Can Make Your Life Count* by Arthur Caliandro. I explained to her that it had been written by a friend of mine with whom I had spent the day. She seemed interested and continued to talk with me. Our conversation evolved from the literary to the personal, and within thirty minutes she had told me her life story, plus her candid evaluation of New York City, where she had attended a seminar on hair styling.

Sensing that she was eager to talk, I asked her about herself. Her name was Cindy, and she worked in Atlanta as a hairdresser. Her childhood was a happy and pleasant one. Her father had served as organist in a number of churches, but now he was divorced from her mother, a break that seemed to be filled with questionable and painful actions on his part.

Cindy and Jim had been married almost a year after living together for four years. Before the minister would perform the ceremony, he required both her and her husband to come to see him for counseling. Jim reacted negatively, fearing that the minister would only reprimand him for living with Cindy before marriage. She persuaded him to meet with the minister, and the encounter had proved positive, with the result that both she and he had been attending church.

I asked her, "What does going to church mean to you?" I hoped she would share with me some of her spiritual pilgrimage. My hopes were not disappointed.

"I go to church almost every Sunday. I love my minister. He helps me so much. He seems to speak right to me every Sunday." She paused and, somewhat distressed, said, "I just don't believe some of the things that they say I must believe to be a member of the church."

"Like what?" I asked.

"I just don't believe that Jesus was born of a virgin. I try to believe it, but my rational mind won't let me. I wish that I could, but I can't."

"Maybe you're beginning at the wrong place. What do you believe about Jesus?" I asked. I wanted her to state her faith more positively, if she had any affirmations she could make.

"I believe that . . ." Her words trailed off. "I guess I ought to start with God," she said. "I'm not too sure what I believe about God."

I listened for quite a while as she walked around her doubts about the reality of God and her longing to believe that God is real and that we can know God's presence in our lives. "Have there been times in your life when you have felt close to God?" I asked.

"When I was a little girl, I felt close to God. I lived in a very safe world my mother and father created for me. They told me about God, and I believed that God was up there looking over me and taking care of me. I have trouble thinking of God like that any more. My mind keeps questioning."

Without rushing her story, I encouraged her to keep

talking about the faith she wished she had. Then I suggested, "Think back over your life and tell me some other times that you have felt close to God."

"I feel close to God in church," she responded. "When I listen to the minister, I seem to hear God speaking to me, but when the service is over, I leave God in the church."

She continued, "I also feel something from the people. It's like there is an electricity in the group when they come together to worship. I feel the presence of God then." She began to feel a little uncomfortable and to back away. "At least, I experience something, and I guess it is the presence of God."

I asked her if there were other times when God seemed near to her. "Yes, when I run. After I have run four or five miles, I feel clean, whole, at peace, and I wonder if God is not a part of that."

She told me that she often prayed on the way to work, hoping that God would make her day better. Then she explained with a radiance in her face that certain of her customers brought her real joy, and she eagerly looked forward to their appointments.

Because Cindy demonstrated such an open spirit, I felt that I knew her in just a matter of minutes. I believed that God was at work in her life in a significant way, and I wanted very much to help her become aware of the presence of God and find the courage to work through her doubts.

Before I tell you how I tried to guide Cindy, let me pick up your story again. We left off with your identifying the major turning points in your journey and asking yourself some important questions about the events of your life. My purpose in asking you to engage in this reflection was to help you become aware of the events of your life and the story that you tell yourself about those events. In the story you tell, you express the meaning of your life as you understand it at this point on the journey.

Let me now guide you in a process of looking for the spiritual dimension of your story. In one sense of the word, your story itself is spiritual because it expresses the meaning of your life. By spiritual dimension, I am referring to the conscious connection of your life story with God. Where has God been at work in the events of your life and the story you tell yourself?

To answer this question, it is necessary for you to understand how you perceive yourself as a person, a human being, and to identify a way that you can begin to refine your perception of God. The spiritual dimension of the journey consists of your understanding of the presence of God in your life. How you perceive yourself and how you perceive God are, therefore, issues of major importance.

Early in this journey narrative I suggested that you were a self-conscious person in whom the physical, emotional, rational, and spiritual unite. You have the capacity to understand all aspects of reality because they reside in you.

Another fact that conditions your life is your finitude. You are a creature limited in time. You had a beginning and you will have an end. Now, in this time, your time, you make this journey.

To a degree beyond my capacity to measure, the awareness of my finitude, I suspect, has fueled a fervent quest for the meaning of my life.

During the first years of life my consciousness, like that of Cindy and all children, was submerged in my parents and the culture that surrounded us. These forces unconsciously determined life, but at twelve years of age I recall falling out of this safe nest. The actual experience of this "fall" was quite painful. It occurred in a flash when my mother asked me, "Where is your knife?"

"At school," I answered.

Since my teacher was also my cousin, my mother probably had inside information on the precise nature of the situation. Actually, my teacher had taken my pocketknife and secured it safely in her locked desk drawer the day she discovered that I had neatly carved B C J on my school desk.

Well, the knife *was* at school, in the desk drawer of my teacher. Mother had a notion that I had purposely misrepresented the truth to her, and she reacted accordingly.

This incident showed me that I was more than an extension of my family. I had the power to contradict what Mother had taught me about honesty. I discovered through this experience a force within me that rebelled against custom, teaching, and tradition. Responding to this negative force left me anxious and fearful.

Besides living in a world limited by time and being able to contradict yourself, you have a deep dimension of your being that is spiritual. The spiritual aspect of your being hungers for meaning that will extend beyond time as well as heal the brokenness that results in guilt and fear. You function on two levels at one time, a conscious and an unconscious level. On the conscious level, you are aware of persons, events, experiences. Your conscious mind deals with what is immediately present to it. This holds true even when memory brings the past to consciousness.

But you have a deeper dimension. At another level, not within your immediate reach, you have a vast store of possibility and potentiality. At this depth you possess in memory your own past. Also, within this depth but not accessible to your immediate vision, or to your grasp, you have a spiritual dimension, a capacity for that which transcends you. I think of this personal unconscious as that part of you that is continually open to the presence of God. In each moment of life the presence of God sustains our being. "In him we live and move and have our being," witnessed the apostle Paul. God sustains and impacts your spirit with the holy presence like waves washing on the beach.

For a healthy spirituality you must also recognize that beyond this deep mysterious self, you are a person who has been shaped by a community beginning with your father and mother and extending to those relatives and friends with whom you shared life. The way you perceive reality was given to you in your earliest relationships in your society of origin. In that community you received your primal images of God. You received an image of yourself. And, quite unconsciously, you adopted goals for your life. Your part in the drama of your life, written by those societal directors, you have played out again and again on the stage of history. In that community you were given a language and the special shades of meaning for your vocabulary. With these tools you question and construct your reality by narrating the significant experiences of your life.

That community also provided you mentors, models who in your earliest encounters displayed a way to "lean into life." In most instances you adopted the values and style of your mentor without realizing how or why. The mentors changed. At one time the mentor was a parent, later on a teacher, then perhaps a preacher. They performed their part in shaping your life and then walked away; their grip on you loosened but your memory of them remains forever strong.

In addition to being a social person, you have the power to transcend yourself and your present situation.

You have demonstrated this power in putting together the structure of your life. You recalled the past, brought it into the present, and reviewed the structure that you have given to the past. Not only can you transcend the present by recalling the past, but you can actually change your perception of the past. A parent, for example, whom you perceived as hating you and deliberately doing harm to you, can be perceived in a new light. You can reinterpret parental behavior in light of a larger vision. This power shows your ability to disengage yourself from destructive experiences and perceptions of the past.

But you also have the power to transcend the present in the direction of the future. You can imagine a different future. You are not bound by your past experiences, or by your genetic inheritances, or by the language and values you have received. You can change!

For example, when Cindy was talking with me about her mistrust of God, I asked, "Do you think that your mistrust of God has any relation to your father's betrayal of you and your mistrust of him?" She had already thought of the question but didn't have an answer. Each of us has the capacity to recall the past, examine it, make new decisions about both our pains and joys, and weave these new meanings into our lives.

I emphasize this possibility because the review of your life may have turned up old experiences that need reinterpretation. Though this task may be painful, it is a necessary one.

My task of reinterpretation has included looking again at my feelings about my father for giving my dog away. My anger, disappointment, and feelings of rejection needed resolution so that I could go forward on this life journey free of that baggage.

The view of human personality I have been describing has several implications for the spiritual journey. First, it suggests that the journey should be taken with seriousness; after all, we make this journey only one time. This view also describes us as persons who have the qualities for spiritual experience—memory, imagination, and intuition. Since persons are created in communities, they require communities in which to grow and develop their spiritual lives. This understanding of human nature makes an encounter with God plausible, if not essential.

Now back to my conversation with Cindy. She clearly indicated to me that she had problems with believing all the things her church required her to believe about Jesus Christ. She also had some questions about the nature of God. At one point I spoke frankly to her. "Cindy, I believe I can see the work of God in your life. I don't mean to impose on your experience a 'God interpretation,' but I really think I see in your life story the evidence of the presence of God. You talk about being near to God in church, feeling God's presence after you have run, thinking that God may be present to you in your customers, and even making an effort to surrender your life to God. I think even your struggle with what you call your 'rational mind' is indicative of God's presence in your life. I would like you to be able to identify the presence of God in your experience, and I have a suggestion that I think will help."

"What is that?" she asked.

"In the Christian tradition we say that God is like Jesus. Begin with this affirmation and read the Gospel of Mark. As you read this one description of Jesus, ask only one question of the text: If God is like Jesus, what is God's nature?" I explained to her that Mark did not begin his report with the story of the virgin birth but focused immediately on the ministry of Jesus.

She said, "I'll do it. I'll read Mark to see what I can discover about God!"

I do not know what Cindy discovered about God as she read the Gospel of Mark. My present concern is what you can discover about God. Your image of God has importance equal to, or greater than, your perception of yourself. Self and God are the major components of the spiritual journey.

If you are still at that stage of your life where you question the actuality of God, assume the possibility that God is and that you wish to discover what God is like. The Bible never seeks to prove the existence of God. All of our efforts to prove this supreme reality will go unrewarded. For the sake of your investigation assume that God is and that God's character is reflected in Jesus of Nazareth. The long tradition of the Christian church stands behind this affirmation. It is not within our power to find God; it is not in us to call God down from heaven. If we make the assumption that Jesus has come to show us God, we will first off find that we are the recipients of a gracious gift.

If God is active in your life, you need clear vision to perceive the divine presence. Moses is an example of what I mean. Recall how Moses, the Israelite, fled from Egypt after killing an Egyptian. He was tending his father-in-law's sheep when a strange thing occurred. He noticed a flaming bush that did not burn out. Turning aside to observe it, Moses heard a voice from the bush, "Moses, Moses. Do not come near. Take off your shoes, for the place where you are standing is holy ground."

Moses did as he was commanded and in that moment realized that he was being encountered by the Holy One, the God of Abraham, Isaac, and Jacob. He was afraid and hid his face. In that encounter the God of whom his fathers had spoken became personally present to Moses. He needed no proofs for the existence of God. This encounter with God carried a conviction within itself; it was self-authenticating. The certainty about God came from this personal meeting with the divine presence.

If you will open yourself to the story of Jesus, you will increasingly become aware of the nature of God as one who comes to us. Your exposure to Jesus will enable you to recognize God in the "burning bushes" of your life.

As you continue to look at Jesus' relation to God, you will see that he depended on God for everything. This fact suggests that all of us are dependent on God for life and breath. Without the presence of God, nothing that is could be. God made everything and God sustains everything. During every moment of our being we exist because God sustains us.

God is personal. God may be more than that, but at least God is personal. We see evidence for that personal nature in God's coming to us in the person of Jesus. In Jesus, God calls us. If we take Jesus' relation to persons as an expression of God, we must conclude that God loves us and cares about our deepest needs.

If we take the life and ministry of Jesus as an expression of God, we begin to suspect that our life journey has a goal. We are not left to the whims of fate, but in gentle, subtle ways Providence directs our course. We, at least, begin to entertain the notion that we do not live in a mechanical, naturalistic world. Rather, we begin to look for the Other who is present to us in nature, coming to us in the events of our lives and expressing a presence through persons.

As we reflect on the mission of Jesus in this world, we cannot avoid the notion that God wills to be known. It was not enough to create the beauty of the world; nor was God satisfied to choose a people and give them a set of rules. God willed for human beings to know God. The God of creation could have remained remote and solitary but chose to come among us.

Every time I visit the beach I fall in love with the gulf again. I don't know all about the gulf—most of it will always remain unknown to me—but I know the gulf. It has a nearness. It washes the beach clean night after night; I can sit in its edge and feel it caress my feet; I can sail over it with carefree ease, and be sung to sleep by the music of it. But it also contains a depth, a mystery that reaches farther than eye can see or ear can hear.

God is like that. God is so vast that we can never think large enough thoughts to contain the divine presence, but God has a nearness. God has come near in Jesus Christ.

That boundless creative ground of everything has come to us in a person, a particular person, Jesus Christ. In Jesus, God has made a statement about God's nature. Not a new set of propositions, not rules, but a person who enfleshes the love and power that created everything and cares for us. Without this revelation in Jesus, God would have remained a vague, impersonal force without a face, without a name.

Make the reading of the scriptures a discipline for your life. In the reading of these stories about Jesus and the life of God's people, your eyes will be sensitized to see the presence of God in your life.

Sometime ago I interviewed a middle-aged couple who had discovered a new depth of meaning in their lives. John had been a land developer in the city. Each project grew larger than the last, and the financial rewards had been generous. Marsha had given him her support and somewhere along the way had begun her own publishing business. The professional success and the affluence that accompanied it did not satisfy the deeper longing of their lives. Through teaching a Sunday school class John began to hear for himself the lesson he taught others. Marsha enrolled in a Bible class and began to discover the ways of God with persons.

As my conversation with Marsha drew to a close, she reflected on her study of the Bible. "You know," she began, "studying the Bible has been so important for me. I am beginning to know Christ well enough to recognize his presence in my daily life." Perhaps you already know much about Christ and his ways with persons, but I am encouraging you to read the Gospel of Mark and later the rest of the New Testament so that you can discern more clearly the presence of God in your life.

You may wonder why I have gone to great length to describe the kind of person who makes the spiritual journey as well as why I have invited the reading of the Gospel of Mark to discover the character of God. The answer is simple. I want you to appreciate the marvelous capacities of the soul to deal with the past, present, and future with imagination and faith. I also want you to have sensitive eyes in this process to discern the activity of God in your life. An interpretation of your natural journey from the divine perspective transforms it into a spiritual journey.

A simple exercise will illustrate what I mean. In the last chapter I asked you to identify the marker events on your journey. Then I asked you to name the space between each of these events. This process provided you with the substance of your life story; that is, the structure of your journey. The discovery of the spiritual dimension of your journey requires the use of your "faith faculty," another name for your creative imagination. Here's how you can use it constructively to get clues about the spiritual dimension of your life.

Choose any one of the spaces between your marker events. Review the actual events that took place in that period of your life. Begin by asking yourself, "Was God possibly working in these events? Why did this event happen to me? How have the events of this period contributed to the meaning of my life?" As you review these experiences, give your imagination freedom to see what God was possibly doing in your life.

For the periods of my life I called "a move to town" and "growing up feeling anxious," I searched the events and wondered where God was in my life. This period consisted of a new school, new teachers, going to church for the first time, my first sweetheart, and hearing of my mother's love. In my creative imagination I saw God placing me in this town so that I could learn about Jesus. My first Sunday school teacher, Mrs. Cooper, taught me to sing "Jesus Loves Me," a simple truth that stayed with me. In this period my mother said to me, "Ben, I will always love you; you cannot do anything that will keep me from loving you." This promise would later become the basis for my understanding, in part, the love of God. How do you see God at work in a segment of your life?

I am not asking you to impose some false interpretation on your experience in order to bolster your faith. Do not spiritualize your life in a way that feels phony; but by the same standard, don't ignore the presence of God that has been active in your life experience. Would it be a serendipity to recognize that God has been shaping your life toward meaning and fulfillment since the day you were born?

Do you recall how Cindy, the young woman on the plane, did not have an awareness of the presence of God in the unfolding of her life drama? Yet, when I asked her a few questions about when she experienced the presence of God, or when God had been nearest to her, she could answer each of those questions. I suspect that her own answers have opened new questions for her and that she has been thinking about other parts of her life. As you reflect on the events of your life, you will begin to make connections between your life story and the presence of God.

This type of reflection may not be new to you. You may have already recognized God in your life story, but now I am asking you to be more intentional and systematic in your reflection. As you consider your entire life in this fashion, you will have a much larger picture of the work of God in the events of your life.

You began with the data of your life and then connected that data with the activity of God. As your spiritual guide, I want to concentrate now on the ways in which you can deepen your awareness of God. This depth cannot be achieved by your own efforts; that would be an old kind of spiritual works for merit. The transformation of consciousness I hope for is a gift, and there are various ways to receive the gift. The next chapter will describe ways that you can be open to receive the gift of God's presence in your consciousness.

Please turn to Appendix B, Exercise 3, "Reflections on Your Journey," for further guidance in realizing how God has been active in your life.

4

Prayer
and the Spiritual Journey

*Prayer is a way to open our lives
to the sacred dimension
of our life journey.*

One of the greatest obstacles on my spiritual journey has been the artificial division of the natural and the spiritual. For a number of years these two aspects of my life opposed each other, surrendered to each other, or occupied nonconnecting rooms. How does the natural life become spiritual and the spiritual life become natural?

When I was a young minister in my second pastorate, about five years out of seminary, I began to be aware of this persistent conflict in myself. On the one hand, I knew the teaching of the Bible and I held a clearly worked-out theology. But on the other hand, I was living my life as a husband, father, and minister in a community. I knew all the right words to say about God and God's relation to the world, and I knew the pain of conflict in my relationships and the suffering experienced in our community, but I did not know how to bring these two worlds together. In retrospect it seems that the resolution to this problem came gradually in two parts.

The first part of the answer was a vision of God as the God of all of life. In the early days of my spiritual journey

God was in heaven and I was on earth. God came to me on special occasions, especially when I had done something wrong. For the most part God was someone to be feared and obeyed. Because of my fear it seemed best to keep God at a distance that only reinforced the contrast between the natural life and the spiritual life.

When I began to read the New Testament with the assumption that God is like Jesus, the negative image of God began to dissolve. The God who is like Jesus Christ not only invites closeness but shows concern for the whole of our life. Thus, nothing in life is unimportant to God.

The second part of the answer to this separation of life into compartments came to me in the discovery of a particular disciplined approach to prayer. The day I was introduced to the experiment in prayer stands out in my memory like a concrete historical marker on the highway. I have returned on numerous occasions to recount the discovery.

I attended a ministers' meeting. During one of the breaks, a fellow minister, Rev. D. K. Christenbury, began telling me about the experience of God that he and several men in his church were having. He said, "We started a prayer group that meets weekly. About half a dozen men meet with me to pray and share our lives. Now we are beginning to experience answers to prayer. People are being healed; some are being changed in other ways." This story so deeply impressed me that a few weeks later I went to visit this pastor.

At the close of our visit he gave me a small booklet, *Teach Me to Pray* by W. E. Sangster. Little did I realize how one hand reaching out to another with a booklet would be such an important marker on my journey. I first read the booklet with little response. After a few weeks I read it again. This time Something spoke to me that called me into a disciplined approach to prayer.

On page 7 of the booklet I came across a structured form of prayer that described how to express Adoration, Thanksgiving, Dedication, Guidance, and Intercession. I reacted negatively to this structure. "How can this man construct a form by which I am to pray?"

Something within spoke. "If your method of prayer is not effective, why not try what someone else suggests?"

"All right," I responded, "I will give you one week to demonstrate what this way of prayer can do." At the end of one week I had already begun to experience the presence of God in my daily life in a new and exciting way. God was no longer held prisoner in the Bible or in my theology. Thoughts and experiences of God began to invade my ordinary day. The wall that separated those two rooms in my life began to be torn down. Life and faith began to merge.

Do not let this brief description mislead you. The separation did not disappear in a few weeks, but I began to discover an approach to life that held out the possibility of integrating these two important aspects of my being.

Before I explain to you how this structured approach to prayer became so important to me in bringing together the natural and the spiritual journey, let me describe a similar pattern of prayer. This is basically the outline I got from Dr. Sangster's book, but I have expanded it in different directions.

Morning Prayer

MEDITATION: Meditation is the act of focusing our attention on God. Get still. Become quiet within. Say to yourself, "I am here to meet God. Nothing else matters for now. God has the place of eminence in my life." Wait until you become centered.

ADORATION: Focus your attention on the greatness of God. Think of the incredibility of God's love. God knows you. God accepts you. God's infinite power, wisdom, beauty are all subjects for adoration. Offer to God the words of praise and adoration that come to mind.

THANKSGIVING: Think of all the things God has given you: the gifts placed in your hands, family, work, health, recreation, a task. All of these are bequests for which to thank God. If you lack these, there are still numerous blessings God has given you.

CONFESSION: Go over your life. Review the events of yesterday. Are there broken places? Did your life betray Christ? Ask his forgiveness and believe now that he does forgive you.

DEDICATION: You have already dedicated your life to God. You have been baptized, confirmed, a member of God's family. If you are married, you are committed to a spouse, also to a vocation. Let God hear the renewed affirmation of your dedication.

PETITION: Petition is the act of asking God for the deepest needs of our lives. Jesus said, "Ask and it shall be given you; seek and you shall find." Because he instructed us to ask for our needs, pray boldly for them.

INTERCESSION: Pray for others. Think of persons in your family, in your church, in your neighborhood who need the love of God. Call their names in prayer and offer them to God. Visualize Christ meeting their needs.

SILENCE: When you have finished interceding, enter into the silence of your own soul. Let God speak. You may hear much. You may hear nothing at all. Give God an opportunity to speak through your imagination. Listen to what arises from your depths.

Take this renewed consciousness into your day.

Prayer in the Evening

Plan to allow ten or fifteen minutes before going to bed to go over the day and prepare yourself for sleep.

First review the events of your day. Think back over the people you met, the tasks you performed, the relationships you had. Do you find any brokenness in your day, any failure to manifest the Spirit of Christ? Any reason to be grateful?

Confess your sins. Offer God your honest confession without becoming morbid or obsessed. Simply confess your sin to God, believing that "if we confess our sins, he is faithful and just to forgive us our sins, and to cleanse us from all unrighteousness" (1 John 1:9).

Surrender yourself to God. Offer God your whole life as you prepare for sleep. Rest in the arms of God knowing that God has claimed you and owned you.[1]

Do you see how this approach to prayer begins to dissolve the tension between the natural and the spiritual? Reflect on each of these movements in prayer as a way of opening your whole life to God and of viewing your life as lived before God.

In *meditation* you turn your attention to God. You probably have an interest in turning toward God because God has already turned to you. Meditation is a knock on the door.

Adoration is the human response to the mystery of God. It is the human response to a glimpse of the Divine.

The act of *thanksgiving* provides an opportunity to inventory all your gifts and to express your gratitude. In so doing you are acknowledging that God is the source of your dearest treasures.

Confession provides a source of healing for the broken places in your life. Important for the unity of faith and life, confession always deals with the real broken-ness of your life.

Dedication brings your whole life before God as an offering.

Intercession defines the depth of your concern for others on the journey, and *petition* expresses the needs you have for making your own journey.

Through the admixture of life and prayer and prayer and life you will begin to discover that prayer is the substance of life, and our lives are forms of prayer.

To expand your awareness of God, begin a time of prayer each day using this format. A few decisions will make the beginning steps easier. Decide on a time and place for your meeting with God. Most persons find the early hours of the day best. The place you choose should be private and free of noise. Resolve that you will engage in this approach for at least a month. Having decided on the time and place with an intentional dedi-cation, even so you are likely to encounter a few prob-lems.

You may begin this experiment in living prayer with high resolve but after a few days find yourself too busy. So you miss a day. Your most important act will be to pick up the discipline the next day. Do not allow your-self to be filled with guilt. Confess your failure and begin again.

You may find it difficult to concentrate on God. Your thoughts will wander to a hundred different distrac-tions—tasks of the day, an ache in your back, the bark of a dog, the ring of the phone, and on and on. . . . Do not chide yourself. Simply and deliberately return your attention to God.

In the early days of this adventure you may find your-self full of doubts. The thought arises, "This act of talk-ing to empty space is the dumbest thing I've ever done!" Don't be afraid of your doubts. Acknowledge them to God with a simple confession, "I am having questions about you and the validity of trying to talk with you about my life." Remember, you can never "shock" God with your confession.

As you continue the experiment in prayer, you will face the issue of surrender. You cannot turn toward God without feeling the call of God to offer yourself. If your commitment to God has been vague, "surrender as much of yourself as you can to as much of God as you understand" today. This act of surrender will open the door to new discoveries.

If you struggle to dedicate yourself to God, talk with God honestly about your difficulty. At least say that you think you would like to make a commitment to God. This response on your part forms a bridge in your consciousness; it is an appropriate first response to the call of God.

This short list does not exhaust the problems confronting a person attempting serious prayer. These distractions are among the first that you will face. As you win a temporary victory over them, others will show themselves.

We have been examining ways of uniting life with God and God with life. Two discoveries are essential for this task: (1) a larger vision of God as the ground of life and (2) a disciplined practice of prayer. After you have engaged in this classical form of prayer for a few weeks, I believe you will begin to experience a new unity of life and God.

If you are the type who has difficulty with structure, another image may help. Offer these prayers through the various faculties of your body. This approach will provide both variety and challenge.

Think of this form of prayer as incarnational prayer. Since the word "incarnation" means endowment with a human body or an appearance in human form, the type of prayer I am advocating breaks down the walls between body and spirit. Think of the different parts of your body as providing ways of prayer. For example, incarnational prayer may begin with the prayer of the lips (words), but it also includes the eyes (vision and images), the mind (ideas and thoughts), the heart (feelings and emotions), the hands (service), the feet (obedience), and the ear (listening).

Picture your prayer as a movement that proceeds from lips to eyes, to mind, to heart, to hands, to feet, and to ears. Every part of the body engages in prayer. First, the prayer of the lips. Verbal prayer is the starting point for prayer. Jesus taught us to pray with words. He said, "Ask and it shall be given you. Seek and you shall find. Knock and it shall be opened unto you" (Matt. 7:7).

You may also pray with your eyes. Visualize your prayers. Leave the world of words and picture your prayers. For example, instead of asking Christ to heal a friend, picture Christ standing beside her bed, stretching out his hand, touching her and making her well. Images precede words and thus may be more effective forms of prayer.

Incarnational prayer includes the prayer of the mind. When you think about God, you are praying with your mind. Every thought of God is a form of prayer. When, for example, you read the Gospel of Mark with the question, "What is God like?" you are praying. Or when you reflect on the call of Jesus, "Come, follow me" (Mark 1:17), and ask questions of it, you are praying. Questions like "What does it mean to follow him? How can I follow him now? What will it require of me to follow him?" are actually alternative forms of prayer.

Another form of incarnational prayer is the prayer of the heart, the prayer of affections and feelings. These prayers stem from deep longings for God. Often these desires, too deep for words, must rely on the Spirit of

God to communicate through us with unutterable sighs (Rom. 8:28–29).

Incarnational prayer requires the prayer of the hands, which unites the feelings of your heart with actions. Prayer with your hands could also be called "doing your prayers." "Doing prayer" is another way of uniting the spiritual with the actual events of our lives.

Consider the prayer of our feet. I think of the feet as members of the body that have the capacity to follow, to obey Christ. When the first disciples left their boats and nets, they followed Jesus. They followed him on foot. Every act of obedience is a form of prayer.

Finally, the prayer of the ear may be the most important aspect of incarnational prayer. The prayer of the ear is the prayer of listening, and we cannot listen unless we are silent. In the silence alone with God, we listen to what God says. Listening, the highest form of prayer, opens us to the mysterious and unfathomable depths of our own being and to the one who sustains all of being.

As you use all your faculties to express the different forms of prayer, increasingly the dividers that separate life into compartments will come down. The masters in the school of prayer often say, "Life is prayer and prayer is life." When prayer and life unite, a person does not work at prayer, it becomes as natural as breathing. An old Jewish proverb says, "The last thing a fish sees is the water." Birds do not notice the air they live and fly in, but deprive them of it for a few minutes and see them flounder. Is that not like God in our lives?

As you begin to live prayer, your conscious life becomes saturated with a sense of the Holy One, and a larger vision of prayer comes to you. This vision fuses life with God and directs you toward living to the glory of God. What is God's glory but God's will being done on earth as it is in heaven? We will have made good progress on our journey when we learn that true prayer seeks to actualize God's intention both in our lives and the larger society.

Do I have a life that is united with God in the fashion I am describing? No, I don't, but I have a picture of it. I have a desire to be more fully open to the divine presence. If this vision seems far removed from your life, please don't be discouraged. It is not yet fulfilled in mine, either, but it points us in the right direction for our lives.

If prayer with the whole person is incarnational prayer, it results in an incarnational life, Christ in us. What is the character of an incarnational life?

An incarnational life is one of conscious response to the initiative of God. Because God wills to be known, God intervenes in the flow of our lives. God comes to us through the events of our lives, through the words of the Bible, the events of biblical history. God also comes to us in the personal caring, rebuke, and challenge of other persons. God's approaches to us are as numerous as the experiences of life.

God also comes to us in the form of another's need. The homeless, the hungry, the sick and lonely bring the divine presence. In that brokenness God waits to be recognized. When we reach out with hands of compassion to minister to those needs, we are making an intentional response to the presence of God. In that simple act Christ becomes present through us.

Our response to this initiative of God forms our prayer. When we say yes to the will of God with our choices, we are praying. Prayer as response takes the form of loving service.

A student came to me for counsel. He was struggling with grades, worrying about preparing for a career, feeling guilty that his life of prayer had deteriorated since entering seminary. Before coming to seminary he had spent time in prayer each morning. He had been disciplined in his response to God.

I invited him to consider his whole life a response to God. Being enrolled in seminary, taking difficult courses in Hebrew grammar and Greek exegesis could be his way of responding to God's initiative. Each time he opens a textbook, he is responding to God. His attendance in each class fleshes out his obedience to God. Each time he opens a book to study, he is saying, "Speak, Lord, your servant hears. Be it unto me according to your will."

One model of response to the initiative of God may be seen in a lowly virgin in Nazareth. The angel of God comes to her. He announces that she is to have a son. She questions. He assures her that nothing is impossible with God. Mary responds, "I am the Lord's servant; may it happen to me as you have said" (Luke 1:38). No greater response to the initiative of God can be imagined. Can we learn to live our lives as response?

The incarnate life of prayer is characterized by loving God with all of your heart, with all of your soul, with all of your strength and loving your neighbor as yourself (Matt. 22:37–39). The thing on which you set your love and affection—that represents God to you. The act of attending, loving, and responding to that object of affection forms your prayer. Whatever, therefore, your heart most deeply desires is your God. When your deepest longing is the knowledge of God and God's purpose for your life, you are offering your profoundest prayer.

The desire of the heart is the prayer of the soul. When Augustine said, "Thou hast made us for thyself, O God, and our hearts are restless until they rest in thee," he described a restless hunger as the source of our urge to pray.

A friend of mine is a missionary in Ecuador. He has

identified with the poor, the dispossessed and power-less people of that nation. Hunger, filth, sickness, and human suffering are the substance of his days. As he travels the countryside, he stops to help a man start his car, he offers a hug to a dirty child who runs to meet him, and he gives food to a hungry mother and her baby.

A visitor asked him, "Why are you burning yourself out in this small country where there is no hope for social reform? Isn't there something more important for you to do?"

My friend answered, "Every person's life is like one tiny grain of sand, and each of us must decide where to lay our grain on the beach of life. I have chosen to lay mine beside these suffering people!" I think he is prayer incarnate!

You will also discover that the incarnate life expresses itself in a studied awareness of who you are. This deepened awareness will clarify in your mind's eye the unique person you are created to be. Every encounter with your true self will evoke a prayer from your heart. To know yourself as you really are is to know your weakness, sin, and finitude. This awareness will turn your mind to God like a magnet spinning a compass.

John Calvin declared:

> Without knowledge of self, there is no knowledge of God. Nearly all the wisdom we possess, that is to say, true and sound wisdom, consists of two parts: the knowledge of God and of ourselves. But, while joined by many bonds, which one precedes and brings forth the other is not easy to discern. . . . No one can look upon himself without immediately turning his thoughts to the contemplation of God. . . . Our very being is nothing but subsistence in the one God.[2]

This interrelatedness of self-knowledge and prayer led Walter Hilton, the fourteenth-century mystic, to say,

"Strain every nerve in every possible way to know and experience yourself as you really are. It will not be long, I suspect, before you have a real knowledge and experience of God as he is."[3]

The students in a course on Christian Discipleship were reporting on their experiences of prayer. One particularly sensitive student said, "I feel guilty thinking about myself so much. We have been tracing the marker events in our lives, the meaning of these events, and how these have shaped us. Shouldn't we be thinking about God instead of ourselves?"

I asked him, "Can we really know the depth of ourself without being driven immediately to God?" These two focuses cannot be separated.

The incarnate life is a transformed life. Prayer releases a power that transforms our thoughts, feelings, desires, and actions. Prayer begins with conversation with God. Through our dialogue with God, the real presence of God becomes manifest in our flesh. I am not saying that we become divine; nor am I pointing to a special kind of humanity in which we cease to be truly human. I claim that God wills to become manifest in human form, in flesh, in us.

This vision of transformation captured Paul's attention and manifested itself in nearly all his writings. He expressed his concern for the Galatian Christians, "I must travail over you until Christ be formed in you" (Gal. 4:19). He prayed for the Ephesians, "that Christ may dwell in your hearts through faith, that you, being rooted and grounded in love, may be able to comprehend with all the saints what is the length and breadth and depth and height and to know the love of Christ which passes knowledge" (Eph. 3:17–18). Paul speaks of his own life in an incarnational image, "I no longer live, but Christ lives in me" (Gal. 2:20).

The incarnate life is one of vision, a vision of a new

heaven and a new earth. With our hearts purified and our visions refined, we live with a hope of what may become, through the generous love of God, the kingdom of God being made actual among us on earth. Urban Holmes says, "The ultimate purpose of prayer is a deepened sharing in God's vision for the world." This visioning prayer means getting to the center from which all things come, and beholding a renewed universe in which all creation participates in God's eternal purpose.

What, then, is an incarnate life of prayer? It is not a continuous search for an exotic, bizarre, ecstatic, miraculous, or emotional experience. This life does not display its piety for others to see. The incarnate life does not use prayer to get what it wills from God. Nor does this life seek to gain from God a power over others. The incarnate life is one of learning to be open to God so that we can learn to love God with all of our hearts; it is to know ourselves as we appear to God; it is to respond to the initiatives of God's grace that shape our lives and transform us so that we participate intelligently in God's plan for the world. This understanding expands the theater of our lives and takes the limits off our personal journeys.

Some time ago while looking through a catalog I stumbled on a list of books about spirituality. Quite accidentally, or should I say providentially, my eyes fell on the name of a book, *Letters from the Desert*. The author, Carlo Carretto, had been involved in the leadership of the church in Italy, and at age forty-four he heard God say, "I do not want your action; I want your prayer."

He felt guided to the desert, the literal desert of sand and sun, of hot days and cold nights. There he joined a contemplative order where he lived, prayed, and served in silence. When I read his first book, it seemed

to me this man wrote looking into the face of God. I
ordered and read everything he has written.

With that personal introduction to Brother Carlo, listen to how he describes his experience of this incarnate
life.

> When anyone asks me, especially after I have come back
> from the desert, "Brother Carlo, do you believe in God?"
> I answer: "Yes, I tell you in the Holy Spirit, I do believe."
>
> And if my questioner's curiosity is aroused, to the
> point of inquiring further: "What evidence do you bring
> forward for asserting so great a truth?" I say, to conclude
> the conversation, "Only this: I believe in God because I
> know him."
>
> I experience his presence in me twenty-four hours out
> of twenty-four. I know and love his word without ever
> questioning it. I am aware of his tastes and preferences,
> his way of speaking, and, especially, his will.[4]

I do not know in my own experience this profound
awareness of God of which Brother Carlo writes, but I
would like to. In my own journey I have discovered the
value of disciplined prayer to sharpen my vision, I have
on various occasions prayed with my whole being, and
I hope as my journey continues that I will receive the
gift of God's presence so that my life can be an expression of the incarnate life.

I am certain of one thing: if we wish to deepen our
sense of God in our journey, we must learn to pray.

*Please turn to Exercise 4 in Appendix B, "Helps with
Prayer," to aid you in thinking through the role of prayer in
your life.*

5

Worship and the Spiritual Journey

Spiritual journeys are made in the midst of a community of persons— living, dead, not yet born.

Sunday morning. Ten forty-five. I was making my way up the steps leading to the sanctuary when I noticed the inscription over the door: "My house shall be called a house of prayer." Musing over the inscription, I entered the rather small sanctuary.

As I was about to sit down with my family, the man in front of us handed me a ball of twine, while holding to the end. He motioned for me to include the other members of my family in the network. About that time I noticed that a web of string connected every person present, even the minister, who was seated with her head bowed prayerfully.

When the next worshiper entered, I passed on the ball of twine, nonverbally repeating the instructions. As the organ chimed the hour of worship, I surveyed the assembly. Here we were, all connected to one another, offering ourselves in concert to God.

Before the formal beginning of worship, the minister rose to give a brief explanation. She began, "You are the body of Christ, each joined to the other. To dramatize our interrelatedness, I ask each of you to participate in this cord web. Think of it as a cord of love that binds each to all and all to God through Christ. The liturgy will form our prayer today, and each part of the order we will share in corporate communion with God." The minister paused, took the two ends of the thread, and tucked them under the cross on the altar. She conducted the entire worship service with the congregation symbolically connected with the twine.

Since that day I have begun to experience worship as a corporate prayer in unison with each brother and sister present. The corporate prayer of the church shapes and supports the private prayer of the individual.

When my private prayer dries up, I am sustained by the prayer of the community. Then I recognize that being a disciple does not depend totally on my faith, but on that of the church. I am on this journey with others who support and care for me. Like a ray of light piercing a dark night, the presence of God illuminates my journey through the experience of worship in a gathered community. Making this journey with others gives me a perspective which enables me to see more clearly my own path. That Sunday morning experience permanently etched in my mind the corporate nature of the journey.

As important as it is, personal communion with God through a disciplined life of prayer must not become a private search for God isolated from the worshiping community. A quest for God that is made in isolation will distort our lives and our relation to God as well as deprive our brothers and sisters of our gifts. When a person says, "I have my time of daily prayer; God meets me in the quiet moments of worship, and I have no need to participate in corporate worship," this person cuts himself or herself off from a great source of strength.

Private prayer finds its deepest significance when it is united with corporate worship. I will explore with you a creative way to relate personal prayer to corporate worship. Prayer, in the fullest sense, must always be understood as our response to the God who wills to be known, who comes to us, and who desires our wonder, praise, and thanksgiving.

Do not pervert the spiritual journey into a private experience of God. Private prayer isolated from corporate worship does not deserve the name "Christian" prayer. The attempt to worship God only in the private sanctuary of our own souls ignores the divine intention of calling a people to worship and obey God. Think what you will be missing if you seek to make the journey alone.

Private prayer, isolated from the community of faith, will miss the intention of Christ. Christ, the head of the church, wills the whole body to be united and mutually nurturing, to mature in his image (Eph. 4:13). If it is the will of Christ, nothing stronger could be said.

Private prayer isolated from corporate worship deforms the body; a member of the body is missing. The missing member creates a gap in the body of Jesus Christ. Imagine a body without an arm or a leg. Would that be a whole body? Your absence from the body will rob it of the beauty and perfection it deserves. By offering yourself to this corporate community, you share in its fulfillment.

Private prayer separate from corporate worship denies the body of Christ your particular gifts that have been given to nurture and fulfill it (Eph. 4:7, 11). The body of Christ requires each gift to complete and nourish itself. Suppose, for example, that you have a gift for encouraging others. When your gift is withheld, members of the community will miss the bright smile and word of affirmation. You yourself are fulfilled when you use the unique gifts that have been given to you.

You need the responses of members of Christ's body

to help you discern his will for you. A spirituality developed in isolation risks deception, lacking the corrective influence of the community. In the community of faith we share our private visions and personal experiences of the grace of God, and the community listens with discerning ears. The community's response enables us to sort out the voice of God from the murmuring of our own unconscious.

I have an urge to change my vocation, for example. An opportunity presents itself. Should I accept it? I seek out two or three members of the church and share my dilemma with them. Because they know me, my gifts, and a few aspects of my history, they can help me discern whether this offer is a call of God. We need the community to help us become mature in our discernment and response to the presence of God. We are to "no longer be children, tossed to and fro" (Eph. 4:14).

I stress the importance of the community of faith because for the first ten years of my spiritual journey I did not recognize how crucial it was for my growth. I was a swashbuckling frontiersman blazing new trails and demonstrating a variety of Christian heroics. This spiritual individualism left me lonely, empty, and feeling that I was always on stage. I was afraid to get too close to people lest they discover that I betrayed the image I wished them to see.

This individualism began to change for me when I experienced the reality of the corporate church—that we are deeply related to one another. The experience that opened this vision for me occurred in a small group of men who met for prayer. I was the young, energetic minister fresh from seminary with all the answers. The seven men from the congregation hardly knew how to pray. We met each Wednesday morning at 6:00 in the back room of a local restaurant.

Over the weeks we made some important discoveries

together as each one told his own story. I discovered that I did not have nearly as many answers as I thought. Because these men had not expected me to be perfect, they were not shocked when I confessed my doubts and failures. As a result I felt more at ease with them and with myself.

When I talked with them about frustrations in the church or in my personal life, they took me seriously. They prayed for me with confidence that God would work in my life. These experiences began to dispel my loneliness.

Then, one morning I had a startling insight. Each of those men had a dominant characteristic. Ed displayed a guileless simplicity; Billy was honest to the bone; Dan had a sense of humor that could lift anyone's spirit; Horace reminded us all of the rock of Gibraltar. Suddenly, as I viewed each of them, I saw a tiny aspect of Christ. None of them had all the attributes of Christ, but each had something unique that he brought to all the others.

Through the years the insight I received in that small group of men has provided me with an image of the church. Expand that tiny vision and you will understand more clearly why I have emphasized that each of us needs all the others in the body of Christ. But even when you recognize the necessity of participating in the community, there still remains the question of how to participate fully in worship. So often the liturgy seems so formal and impersonal.

"How do we combine personal prayer with corporate worship?" The liturgy bridges personal and corporate prayer. The corporate worship of God is corporate prayer; and the liturgy provides the structure of the corporate prayer.

In somewhat the fashion that I guided you through an approach to personal prayer, I will give you a prayer perspective on corporate worship. First, corporate prayer requires personal preparation for praying the liturgy. Preparation for worship occurs in a daily life of prayer. This preparation cannot occur at 10:45 A.M. on Sunday. Personal preparation includes a recognition that we are part of a larger fellowship, the body of Christ; a recognition of God's gifts to us; learning to image Christ in the community; and looking to Christ as the leader of worship.

Living the adventure daily with Christ is the only adequate preparation for worship. During the week we greet each day with the expectation that Christ will speak to us, through us. We listen for his voice in our conversations with friends. We seek to trace his footprints on the streets we travel to work. We trust that through our choices and actions he is presenting himself to the world again. We strive for our whole being to become a prayer. We pray not only with our lips but with our hands, our feet, and our heart. We hope to become an incarnate prayer.

Richard Foster, author of *Celebration of Discipline*, tells how he sought to "pray without ceasing." For a whole year he tried to pray constantly during the week. "The only thing," says Foster, "that I learned from that experience was that I found that the single greatest change in my experience was a new expectancy in worship."[1]

Our preparation also includes a recognition of our essential unity in the body of Christ. We are not solitary Christians. Even when we are separated in daily life, we are united with the body. The Spirit creates and maintains the body of Christ and connects each to the other.

Every morning when my family leaves the house for work and school, we separate ourselves from one another during the day; but this in no way destroys the family. While we are apart from one another, we still belong together. Each evening we gather for dinner and conversation, affirming again our togetherness. Worship is the gathering of the church to affirm that we belong together even when we are separated.

In your preparation realize also the purpose of the gifts of the Spirit. According to Paul, each of us was given a gift of the Spirit when we were baptized into the body of Christ. To one person the Spirit gives wisdom; to another, knowledge; to another, faith; to another, the gift of miracles, and so forth (1 Cor. 12:8–11). Your gift has been given to use in building up the whole body of Christ. "To each is given the manifestation of the Spirit for the common good" (1 Cor. 12:7). Therefore, your gift must not be withheld from the other members of the body of Christ.

What happened to me in that small group of men can occur in every worship service. The vision of Christ's presence enhances worship for all persons. What would happen if each of us creatively imaged the gathering of the people as the coming together of the actual body of Jesus Christ? While Christ is no longer here in his own flesh, he lives in our flesh. None of us possesses Christ fully. We have only fragments of his presence in our lives. Only in union with others do we become a complete body.

In the communion of the body of Christ, there are two movements: vertical and horizontal. In the vertical movement we are opened to God; in the horizontal we reach out to a brother or a sister. The minister in my opening story endeavored through the twine to help her congregation visualize this interconnection of the human and divine. This unity in Christ transforms not only worship but our lives as well.

As a final act of preparation for worship, look to Christ to lead the worship service. Enter into that sacred place with the vivid expectation that Jesus Christ will appear in the minister! Christ will be present to lift his arms and beckon us into the presence of God. Can we hear the voice of Jesus Christ speaking through this human voice? Can we see through the minister the presence of Christ among us?

Richard Foster believes that just a few persons entering into a worship service fully prepared to worship God can change the whole atmosphere of the service. Not all the participants have to be fully prepared, in order for the Spirit of Jesus Christ to permeate and transform a service of worship. What a challenge to the spiritually perceptive!

Before examining the liturgy as corporate prayer, think how closely the corporate worship of God is related to our personal journey. Corporate worship constantly reminds us that we journey with others. The journey each makes is personal but not private. The affirmation of faith, the hymns, and even the sacred scriptures continue to remind us that our personal journeys are grounded in a larger journey, the history of God's people. In this historical community we find a foundation, boundaries, and also companions.

After preparation for the corporate worship of God, we enter God's house and offer ourselves as God's people. The question still looms before us—how do we, so many and so diverse, become the one Body of Jesus Christ? How does Christ take shape among us in our corporate worship?

The answer: miracle, mystery, and gift. The coming together of the body in unity can be nothing short of miraculous. The unity arises out of the mystery of God whose presence is graciously offered to us. By the miraculous action of the Holy Spirit, these diverse, solitary individuals are welded together into the body of Jesus Christ.

This mystery occurs through memory and imagination. We who know Jesus recall how he has come to us before. Just as the disciples remembered how he had come to them by the lake or at the meal in the upper room or outside the garden tomb, we, too, remember those times and places when Christ manifested himself to us. This active memory of the presence of Christ plus the action of the Holy Spirit on our imagination enables us to recognize his presence among us again.

This actualization of the Body of Christ is aided by our anticipation. As the body gathers, the Spirit acts through our anticipation to become present through faith. We expect Christ to come. As the early church expected him to meet with them at the sacred meal, we expect him to speak through the Word. This anticipation draws us into the future and toward the ultimate fulfillment of the Body of Christ. Today he comes in the Spirit. He heals and nurtures his body. But our expectation will be fulfilled when he comes at the climax of history, when our anticipation is realized in a face-to-face meeting with the Lord.

Christ today takes shape among us through the liturgy—the form of corporate prayer. This order has deep roots in the cultures of humankind as well as the collective unconscious of the church. While the form of our corporate prayer does not make prayer vital, we must recognize that the order is more than an accident. The inspiration of God's Spirit, plus the long experience of God's people, has created the elements, form, and sequence in the liturgy. It has been repeatedly tested, re-formed, and shaped until its essential elements have been etched in the deep memory of the church. (I am writing out of a Reformed perspective. Because of our diversity, some will have a much more formal liturgy, while others will be freer. I suggest you adapt the following according to your background and tastes.)

The church has learned that it prays only at the invitation of God; in response to the invitation, praise only is appropriate; the immediacy of the holy evokes the confession of sin. With clean hands and pure hearts created by the forgiveness of sin, the people are liberated to hear God speak. Hearing God demands response—the offering of self. This sequence of experience has been forged in the furnace of holy experience.

The form of the liturgy corresponds to the experienced reality of life. Even those who have not been reared in a liturgical tradition have a longing for the reality it expresses. A friend from a less formal order of worship shared with me his weariness with worship focused on preaching and decision to the neglect of the pure worship of God. Recently he had been attending a liturgical church. "How deeply," he said, "the liturgy speaks to me. I have a hunger to participate in the church's long, historical act of worship." As we grow older and more experienced in the worship of God, I suspect that we are all drawn by the Spirit into the deep, rich tradition of Christian worship.

The liturgy has profound meaning for us because it is grounded in our essential nature. We are fragile, finite individuals who need to be connected to God. The liturgy provides a form through which we encounter God. It opens the way for spontaneous expressions in silence, in acts of prayer and praise, but its primary intention is to escort us into the immediate presence of God.

Think of the order of worship as corporate prayer. How can each element guide us in corporate prayer? I will make some suggestions to help you appropriate this idea in relationship to parts of the liturgy.

In the CALL TO WORSHIP, the minister re-presents Jesus Christ. We listen to the minister's invitation as the invitation of Christ himself, calling us into the presence of

God. He calls us from the world of created things to the source of all things.

"Enter into his gates with thanksgiving, and into his courts with praise: be thankful unto him, and bless his name. For the LORD is good; his mercy is everlasting; and his truth endureth to all generations. Let us worship God."

Hear these words as the invitation of Christ to each member of his body.

When we enter the "silence of the sacred," the Holy opens to us. In the presence of God, the Holy One, we meet our Creator—the one who has imagined and called forth our very being, the one from whom all things have originated—we meet our sustainer, who holds us in being every moment of our lives. God never leaves us; God does not lose one of us; we meet the One who providentially directs the affairs of our life. The awareness of standing in the presence of God spontaneously evokes our praise. No other response is as appropriate for us as a HYMN OF PRAISE like this:

Praise to the Lord, the Almighty

Praise to the Lord, the Almighty, the King of creation!
O my soul, praise him, for he is your health and salvation!
All you that hear, Now to his temple draw near,
Joining in glad adoration!

. . . .

Praise to the Lord! O let all that is in me adore him!
All that have life and breath, come now with praises before him!
Let the Amen Sound from his people again:
Gladly always we adore him. Amen.

In the presence of God, how can we withhold the CONFESSION OF SIN? We are driven not only to confess our personal sins but our corporate state of sin. Calvin reminds us that we cannot encounter the presence of the Holy God without immediately thinking of our sinfulness and need of confession. Nor can we face our sinfulness without immediately thinking of God. Confession is the appropriate response to a personal encounter with the Holy One. Let your heart confess sincerely.

Listen to the WORDS OF ASSURANCE. Christ speaks these words to us, assuring us that we are accepted. We are forgiven. We are made right with God.

"If we confess our sins, he is faithful and just to forgive us our sins, and to cleanse us from all unrighteousness." Believe the good news.

"Neither do I condemn you. Go and sin no more."

As the body of Christ bound together in love by the Spirit, we join with the people of God through all the ages singing the "Gloria." This RESPONSE was created in the consciousness of the church more than seventeen centuries ago. Today we join the long procession in a chorus echoing:

"Glory be to the Father, and to the Son, and to the Holy Ghost. As it was in the beginning, is now, and ever shall be, world without end. Amen. Amen."

Having confessed to Almighty God, picture the body of believers before the majesty of God LISTENING FOR THE WORD OF GOD. The invitation into God's presence, the offering of praise, the confession of our sin, and the acceptance of pardon free us to become receptive. Eagerly we wait to hear God speak both through the scriptures and the contemporary words of the minister.

Thus, when the minister invites us to pray before the reading of the Word, we ask the Holy Spirit to breathe on the words of the scripture, that they may come alive in our imagination. We can think of the Spirit's presence as a neon light, illuminating the scriptures and causing them to glow with divine light.

In the reading of the Old and New Testament scriptures, we listen for God to speak. God does speak. God speaks a new word to direct the Body of Christ in service.

We listen, too, for God's word in the SERMON. The preacher of the Word lives among the people, sensing the movement of the Spirit in us and in our worlds. In the solitude of the study the minister reads, listens, ponders, and prepares to interpret and speak God's Word to the people. And we pray that the Spirit that illumines the written word will make the minister's human words the Word of God to us.

How do we pray after the sermon has concluded? How impossible to hear God speak without responding! So we respond with confession and commitment.

The living Word of Christ calls forth our confession of faith in Christ. When the Holy Spirit acted on the consciousness of Peter, he said, "Thou art the Christ, the Son of the Living God" (Mark 8:29). We respond to God with the CONFESSION:

> I believe in God the Father Almighty, Maker of heaven and earth; And in Jesus Christ His only Son our Lord; who was conceived by the Holy Ghost, born of the Virgin Mary, suffered under Pontius Pilate, was crucified, dead, and buried; he descended into hell; the third day he rose again from the dead; he ascended into heaven, and sitteth on the right hand of God the Father Almighty; from thence he shall come to judge the quick and the dead.
>
> I believe in the Holy Ghost; the holy catholic Church; the communion of saints; the forgiveness of sin; the resurrection of the body; and the life everlasting. Amen.

We also respond to God with our PRAYERS for the nation and the peoples of the world. The petitions of our community unite our consciousness with the needs of the world.

"Lord of all the worlds that are, Savior of men and women: we pray for the whole creation. Order the unruly powers, deal with injustice, free and satisfy the longing peoples, so that in freedom your children may enjoy the world you have made, and cheerfully sing your praises; through Jesus Christ our Lord. Amen."

After the prayers, our response becomes tangible in the passing of THE PEACE, an enactment of the vision of the connectedness of Christ's body. As members of one body and members one of another we reach out and touch. Not only does the ordained priest of God say the word of forgiveness, but all of us as the priests of God affirm to each other the acceptance, forgiveness, and reconciliation of God.

The offering permits us to make a tangible response to God. The offering symbolizes the self—our being. When, therefore, we place an offering of money in the plate, we symbolically place ourselves in the hand of God.

In a children's sermon, the minister dramatically illustrated this point. A three-year-old girl was instructed to sit down in the offering plate. The minister lifted the plate with her in it and placed it on the Communion table. He then said to the people, "This is what it means to make your offering to God."

The PRAYER OF THANKSGIVING and the LORD'S PRAYER are essential parts of the liturgy as we express gratitude and appreciation for all the blessings in our life.

Jesus said, "As the Father has sent me, even so send I you" (John 20:21). From the Mount of Ascension, the last words of Jesus were, "And you shall be witnesses unto me, both in Jerusalem and in Judea, and in Samaria, and unto the uttermost parts of the earth" (Acts 1:8).

The COMMISSIONING HYMN provides a transition from our response to him in the sanctuary to our being sent forth to respond to him in society. Our prayer in this hymn moves from the active praise of God to the reception of God's call. Our attention begins to shift from God in the church to God in the world. The image for such a movement is our walking forth from the sanctuary, filled with the consciousness of being sent by God. Listen to that charge in this hymn:

A Charge to Keep I Have

A charge to keep I have, A God to glorify,
A never-dying soul to save, And fit it for the sky.

To serve the present age, My calling to fulfill;
O may it all my powers engage To do my Master's will!

Arm me with jealous care, As in Thy sight to live;
And oh, Thy servant, Lord, prepare A strict account to
give!

Help me to watch and pray, And on Thyself rely,
And let me ne'er my trust betray, But press to realms on
high. Amen.

The final CHARGE of God to the people, spoken through the lips of the minister, is "Depart in peace to serve in love." We are sent forth to do the work of God in all our relationships. This commission suggests the prayer of the hands and of the feet in obedient service to Jesus Christ as Lord.

Finally, the BENEDICTION communicates the promise of God. In these words the minister reassures us that God will be with us. We will become active participants in life, living letters of God to the world, bearers of Jesus

Christ in our social milieus. We depart to engage life with the confidence that God is with us.

What would it mean if the church gathered regularly to pray the liturgy with understanding? What could renew the corporate life of the church more quickly? Where would there be greater inspiration for the individual journey?

If two or three persons can change the atmosphere of a worship service, what type of spiritual explosion would occur if all the worshipers truly prayed the liturgy? Would not the electricity of the divine presence spark the service? No person could enter the house of God without sensing the living presence of Christ. Think what corporate prayer can mean to your journey and to that of others.

Let us pray the liturgy—and live it daily!

Please turn to Exercise 5 in Appendix B, "Liturgy as Prayer," for suggestions about corporate prayer in the liturgy of your church.

6

Getting the Journey
in Focus

*The spiritual journey leads inward
to our depths, demanding an acceptance
of ourselves as we really are.*

"Can you help me with my spiritual life?" asked the young journeyer.

"I don't know, but I'll be glad to try," I responded. "What seems to be going on with you?"

"I am concerned about growing in my relationship with Christ. I have committed myself to him. I pray. I spend time reading the Bible. I try to manifest his love for people. With all the efforts I don't feel my discipleship to be very good."

"What is the focus of your life?" I asked.

"That's just it. I don't seem to have a clear focus. I give attention to prayer for a while. Then I devote myself to reading the Bible until that grows dull. I try working on my relationship with my wife."

"There is certainly nothing wrong with any of those goals," I commented.

"But I feel so fragmented," my friend responded.

"What is one thing big enough to give your life focus?" I asked.

"Focus? What do you mean by focus?"

"The point of focus is that place where rays of light converge. Do you recall when you were in elementary school taking a magnifying glass and focusing the rays of the sun on a piece of paper until it caught fire?" I asked.

He nodded.

"Every life needs a focus, a center in which all experience converges. Without this focus a journey loses its definition and becomes blurred and hazy."

"What is the focus for the journey with God?" he asked.

Before dealing with this serious question, let me point out how Jesus emphasized the importance of clarity about this issue. He said, "Blessed are the pure in heart, for they shall see God" (Matt. 5:8).

What did Jesus mean? Does Jesus mean sexual purity? Does he mean purity of motive? Purity means without foreign substances, to be one thing, unmixed like pure water, pure gold, pure air. To be pure is to be without alloy.

Purity of heart is a different metaphor for emphasizing "focus."

"Purity of heart," says Søren Kierkegaard, "is to will one thing." What is the one thing that is to be willed? That is the question of my young friend who was searching for help with his journey.

Jesus taught that "no one can be a slave to two masters; he will hate one and love the other; he will be loyal to one and despise the other. You cannot serve God and money" (Matt. 6:24). Jesus indicated that persons cannot have two focuses if they intend to serve God with their whole heart.

Our God is a jealous God who says, "You shall have no other gods before me." No person can embody two ultimate loyalties. God rejects a mixed loyalty.

With another metaphor Jesus makes clear the necessity of focus when he says, "The eyes are like a lamp for the body. If your eyes are clear, your whole body will be full of light; but if your eyes are bad, your body will be in darkness. So if the light in you is darkness, how terribly dark it will be!" (Matt. 6:22-23). Does this statement shed any light on the confusion in the life of the journeyer searching for a new depth in his relation to Christ? Without a clear focus life is blurred.

In this analogy of the eye Jesus places the problem in human perception. Because of our unfocused lives, we do not have a clear perception of life, or of God's will. If we have a diseased eye, according to Jesus, our lives are distorted and thrown into chaos. A person may suffer three diseases of the eye that cause it to function improperly: myopia, hyperopia, and astigmatism. Myopia causes us to give our attention to matters at hand with no perspective on the future. Hyperopia causes us to be so obsessed with distance, the future, that the present passes unnoticed. Astigmatism blurs the perception of everything. A diseased eye leaves the person without a sense of direction. Blindness is, therefore, an apt metaphor for spiritual malfunction.

Jesus said, "If the eye is clear, the whole body will be full of light." A sound eye, free of foreign matter, can focus on the one thing at hand necessary for a whole life.

Jesus illustrated the kind of problem that arises when our vision is not clear. "Why, then, do you look at the speck in your brother's eye, and pay no attention to the log in your own eye? How dare you say to your brother, 'Please, let me take that speck out of your eye' when you have a log in your eye? You hypocrite! Take the log out of your own eye first, and then you will be able to see and take the speck out of your brother's eye" (Matt. 7:3-5). You remove the obstruction from your own eye by dealing with the barriers in your life; for example, misplaced loves that keep you from the central focus for your life.

What is the focus for our life's journey? What is the single vision, the purity of heart to will one thing, the speck-free eye?

To will God's will.

Nothing in the journey equals this commitment. "In whatever circumstances I find myself, I will God's will." When Jesus' disciples asked him to teach them to pray, he said, "When you pray say, 'Thy kingdom come, thy will be done, on earth as it is in heaven'" (Matt. 6:9–10). This is the central focus of the spiritual journey.

Kierkegaard's unity of will calls for the elimination of all other loyalties. His dictum may be rewritten: "Purity of heart is to will the will of God alone." A disciple of Kierkegaard's says, "Purity of heart is an uncluttered intention to know the will of God."

Jesus' metaphor of clearing the eye suggests an active involvement in emptying our lives of alien loves, of seeking healing for our diseases so that we may focus our vision on the eternal and necessary. Christ calls us to an absolute devotion to God. With respect to choice, Thomas Green says, "We can have many loves in our life, but only one center, one sun around which all our loves are satellites."[1]

My young friend grasped the implications of this central focus. "I gather from your response," he began, "that the focus of a Christian's life is not on prayer or Bible study, but on doing the will of God." He had understood my idea. This emphasis on the will of God does not imply that prayer and Bible study are unimportant, just that they provide help in discerning and doing the will of God.

In Jesus Christ we have a perfect model of a person with clear vision, a unified will, a focus. At the beginning of his ministry Jesus had his singular loyalty to God tested. The tempter sought to turn Jesus from the will of God. Jesus refused the tempter's offer by affirming, "Man shall not live by bread alone, but by every word that proceeds out of the mouth of God." He said, "You shall not tempt the Lord your God." In an act of ultimate loyalty to God, he said, "You shall worship the Lord your God and him only shall you serve." Jesus demonstrated a singular commitment to do the will of God. "I came not to do my own will, but the will of him who sent me" (John 4:34).

In his hour of struggle in Gethsemane he prayed, "Nevertheless, not what I will but what you will" (Matt. 26:39). Offered in the face of his death, this prayer signals a life ending as it had begun with absolute dedication to the will of God.

For this life, more fitting words could not be said than "Into your hands I commend my Spirit. It is finished." Jesus had finished his journey doing the will of God from the beginning to the end. He had found the focus for his life and thereby demonstrated to us what ours should be.

Jesus discovered the secret. "Not my will but thine be done." How do we overcome the distractions that hinder us? My friend Arthur Caliandro, minister at the Marble Collegiate Church in New York City, tells a simple story that may point us in the right direction.

Three boys were playing in a snowy field. The snow was deep, and they were having a great time rolling in it. A neighbor paused to watch them, then called out, "Hey, kids, would you like to have a race? I'll give a prize to the winner."

A race seemed like a good idea to the boys, so they gathered around the man to get their instructions. "The winner," he said, "will not be the one who runs fastest, but the one who runs the straightest line. I'll go to the other side of the field; when I give a signal, you race to me."

He went to the other side of the field and shouted, "On your mark, ready, set, go!" The boys took off. The first one looked at his feet as he ran to make sure that they were pointing straight ahead. The second, worrying about how straight the boys on either side of him were running, tried to line himself up with them. But the third youngster understood the game. He kept his eyes fixed on the man at the other end of the field. He had his eye on the goal. He didn't waver from a straight course, and he won the race.

The other boys fell victim to two common problems encountered on the spiritual journey. The first is the problem of self-consciousness, especially as it manifests itself in feelings of inadequacy. The journey is never made in our own strength but in that which faith supplies. The second problem is too much concern with how others are making the journey. Each of us has his or her own path to follow. We must not try to imitate another.

When we will the will of God, the task does not become easy for us. I find the common experiences of life keep getting in my line of vision. Someone pushes in line before me at the grocery. Quick as a flash, my anger rises, and I feel like booting that person out of the store. From my past, memories arise that haunt me with failure that cannot be corrected. I stand before the mirror to see the result of my overindulgence in food. My mind wanders toward the future, abandoning the tasks at hand. How does a serious journeyer overcome these distractions?

As you can see from my confession, I do not have the problem licked. I take courage in the realization that a goal large enough for my whole life will take my whole life to attain. After more than thirty-five years of being on the journey, I am chiefly concerned with realizing

God's will just a bit more each day. Perfection is not my concern.

Maybe you have just begun to take this spiritual journey seriously, and you are asking, "How do I get started with focusing my will in the will of God?"

You can profitably take inventory of the person you are at this present moment. The self who lives before God here and now composes the essential element in this journey. To get your vision clear as to who you are at this point will make the remainder of the journey much simpler. What do you need to know of yourself to begin clarifying your vision?

Self-knowledge must include who you are physically. Take a look at your physical being, acknowledge it, and confess to yourself your feelings about your body. The body provides a bridge between the inner world of images and feelings and the external world of things and relationships.

You are more than a body; you are a self that has been formed by all the experiences that stand behind you. Honestly face your feelings about yourself and acknowledge them to God. Self-perception greatly influences God-perception.

Your chosen values also tell you a great deal about who you are. Review the things that are important to you. Look at your commitments. What commands your loyalty? Do not deceive yourself.

The significant persons in your life define in part who you are. Who are they, and what do they mean in your life?

How you invest your time indicates another piece of your identity. In becoming aware of who you are, look at how you have invested yourself. What kind of work did you choose to do? How do you spend your non-working time?

Finally, look at your picture of the future. Where are you going in your life? What is your destiny?

This investigation of your life will put you in touch with the formative influences in your life at the present. As you become conscious of all these dimensions of your life, do not judge yourself. Do not permit guilt or grief to overwhelm you. This is your life. Be grateful for your one and only life. Offer it to God with the confession, "This is the person that I am today, and I seek to know and do your will."

I have suggested that you make this journey into the core of your life because of the significance of an experience I had twenty years ago. At that time I felt very much confused about myself, my relation to God, and the clarity of my vocation. I wondered if I could continue as a minister of God.

Then I began to make the great discovery of the love of God. After having preached God's love to others for more than ten years, I finally began to believe that God loved me.

With a growing confidence in that love, I longed to permit it to soothe some sore spots in my life. So, in a fashion similar to the one I have suggested to you, I began to review my whole life. In my memory I returned to the earliest days of my life. I identified all the things that I feared, those that embarrassed me; I uncovered parts of my past I had never acknowledged to another human being.

One by one I brought these memories into the brilliant light of the presence of God and kept confessing, "God, this is Ben Johnson. This is who I am. I actually did these distasteful things. You love me."

Again and again the word of assurance came to me, "Yes, I really love you. I love the real you. I love you as you are."

Those distant parts of myself, so carefully hidden in

the closed chambers of memory, I called up and looked each one straight in the eye. I said to each part of myself that I had feared, "I will face you before God. God will forgive me and heal me."

Day after day, in my time of prayer, I proceeded through the dark as well as the bright places of my past. When I had completed the journey, I had said everything to God about myself that I knew to say. God met my confessions with unconditional acceptance.

As a consequence of the confession of myself, I came into a deeper awareness of who I was and a deeper acceptance of myself as a forgiven person. My fragmented parts found their way back together. I was healed of much of my fear and doubt. Never after that have I felt an urge to hide from God. I no longer have a fear of being found out. God knows me, and I know that he knows all about me. I felt positively accepted at the core of my life.

Through this conscious acknowledgment of my whole self, my life came together. My fragmentation began to dissolve into unity. The walls in the compartments separating faith and life began to crumble. A wellspring of joy burst forth and flooded my consciousness. I will always be grateful for the gift of courage that enabled me to take this journey into my shadow self.

Do you want to know the person you really are? A friend of mine cautioned, "Do not think that all persons want to know themselves. To be honest, the very thought of facing myself scares the wits out of me." You may have the same fears, but be assured that none of the things within you will disappear by pretending they are not there!

If you intend to make this journey into your real self, just a word of caution. Do not make this solitary journey without the assurance of God's unconditional love. In Jesus' dealing with broken persons, we glimpse the

gracious nature of God before whom we are acknowledging our true life.

A paralytic was brought to Jesus by four friends. The
paralytic did nothing: he did not get himself to Jesus; he
made no confession. Jesus, seeing the faith of the
man's companions, said, "My son, your sins are forgiven." Forgiveness came not because of the efforts of
the man in need but from the graciousness of God. The
exposure of ourself to God is enough to invoke God's
love.

The gracious nature of God also appears in Jesus'
encounter with a leper. No one represents alienation,
hopelessness, helplessness like the leper. He said to
Jesus, "If you want to, you can make me whole!"

Jesus responded, "Of course I want to. Be whole."

This reply, "Of course I want to," reveals the utter
willingness of God to respond to our need no matter
how deep.

In another meeting Jesus made the point of God's
unconditional acceptance. A woman apprehended in
the act of adultery was brought to Jesus. To her accusers, Jesus said, "Let him who is without sin among you
cast the first stone." In the deafening silence that followed, the accusers exited. Jesus said to the woman,
"Where are your accusers? Is there no one to condemn
you?"

"No one, sir," she answered.

In one short, penetrating statement Jesus made clear
the unconditional acceptance of God. "Neither do I
condemn you. Go and sin no more" (John 8:11). God's
attitude of no condemnation provides the courage for
us to encounter the darkness in our soul. This grace
becomes a companion to walk with us; a light to make
plain our way; a balm to heal our wounds.

In Jesus Christ we are shown quite clearly that God
is for us. There is no question. The one who has come

among us, lived as a human, offered himself unswervingly to God's purpose, has said for all time, "I love you. I accept you."

The unacceptable in and among us—the paralytic, the leper, the adulteress—have all been accepted in spite of their unacceptability. We cannot commend ourselves to God; we need not commend ourselves to God. We have been commended by Jesus Christ. "But God shows his love for us in that while we were yet sinners Christ died for us" (Rom. 5:8).

Because God's absolute knowledge has been conditioned by unconditional love and undeserved acceptance, God can never be shocked by the darkest darkness in our soul. God knows us. God knows all our wild imaginings and the worst words our lips could ever speak. And still God loves us.

No story in the Bible dramatizes this truth more clearly than the return of the prodigal. The younger brother took his inheritance, journeyed into a far country, and wasted his resources seeking thrills. Not even having food to satisfy his hunger, he decided to return to his father's house. Before leaving the far country, he rehearsed his confession, "I will say to my father, 'Father, I have sinned against heaven and in your sight. I am not worthy to be called your son. Make me as one of your hired servants.'" Day after day, as he journeyed home, he repeated the confession.

When he arrived at his father's house, the father came out to meet him. The son began his well-practiced confession, "Father, I have sinned." The father, ignoring his confession of failure, said to the servant standing by, "Bring forth the best robe and put it on him. Put a ring on his hand and shoes on his feet, for this my son was dead and is alive. He was lost and now is found."

In this encounter the father demonstrated a holy indifference to the confession. The son had come home;

he presented himself to the father. The act of turning toward home was the confession of his life. Possibly this episode reminds us that we have a much deeper need to confess than God has to hear our confession.

The assurance of this unconditional love will give you the courage to make the journey inward. You, like my friend who confessed her fear of this journey, will find a constant supply of God's loving acceptance as you frankly acknowledge the dark side of your existence.

Do you now see why self-knowledge is necessary if you are to will the will of God? Without this depth encounter with yourself and with the grace of God, two fears will constantly plague you: the fear that you are unacceptable to God and the fear that God wills the unacceptable for you. The acknowledgment of your life before God dissolves both these fears. The fear of your dark side is dispelled by the assurance of God's unconditional acceptance, and an assurance of God's unconditional love diminishes the fear of God's will!

I once met a man whose attitude and behavior, more than that of any person I have ever met, provided a shining example of this focused life. I first met him through a book he wrote, *Why Am I Afraid to Tell You Who I Am?* I found John Powell's insights extremely helpful. Immediately I wished to meet him. Years passed—ten, to be exact. Then one evening I found myself in Chicago sitting at dinner with John Powell. I listened attentively as this Jesuit priest joyfully described the acts of God in his life.

One of his experiences models a focused life. When he was a young man just finishing seminary, John made a trip to Rome for an audience with the pope. Following this meeting, he visited Padre Pio, a priest in a small village south of Rome who had received the stigmata, the five wounds of Christ.

The time with Padre Pio passed quickly. Afterward, John Powell was browsing in a gift shop in the village.

The saleswoman asked, "Have you been to see the Padre?"

Powell nodded and continued looking around the shop.

"Did he give you a blessing?" she inquired.

"Well, no. Actually, he didn't," Powell responded.

"He is my spiritual director, and I see him every month. Would you like me to commend you to him?" she asked.

"Yes, yes indeed. I would appreciate it very much."

In a few days Powell returned to the United States and made the terrible discovery that he had a serious eye disease for which no cure was known.

"Why did this happen to me? Why, at this time in my life, at the beginning of my ministry, did God permit this illness to happen to me?" Powell questioned.

His mind raced back to the little village, to Padre Pio, and the woman in the gift shop. Had she commended him to the Padre? He wrote to inquire.

"Yes!" She had commended him, but the Padre had never made any response after her commendation.

Perplexed, Powell consulted with the mystical theologians. "What does it mean that she commends me to the Padre and he remains silent?" The theologians answered, "Either it means that you are so good you don't need a blessing, or so bad there's no hope for you." Dissatisfied with their answer, Powell wrote to the Padre.

Dear Padre, he began, *some months ago I came to see you. You did not offer me a blessing. The lady in the curio shop has commended me to you on numerous occasions. You have said nothing. In the meantime, I have discovered that I have a serious eye disease and I am progressively going blind. What must I do?*

A few weeks later Powell received a handwritten letter from the Padre. It contained only one sentence.

Remember, the transforming prayer is, "Thy will be done."

John Powell heard in this response the call of God. He surrendered himself to God. "Thy will be done, in me, now. Blindness or sight, thy will be done."

This prayer of abandonment has so gripped the mind and heart of John Powell that in his every conversation, you often hear him repeat, "His will be done." In a dimension of his being deeper than consciousness, he has learned the complete focusing of his life in the will of God.

John Powell still has his vision.

Please turn to Exercise 6 in Appendix B, "Writing a Confession," for guidelines in making your own confession of your life.

Appendixes

Appendix A

Journaling, an Important Tool for the Spiritual Journey

The spiritual journal finds a new importance in modern-day spirituality. We will explore a number of possibilities for its use as an aid to spiritual growth.

The spiritual journal records our spiritual pilgrimage; it becomes a place to meet God by listening to the data of our outward and inward life. Here we record the meaning of these data and integrate their significance into our life.

The journal provides a record of our perceptions of God's intervention in our life. This material describes the outer events of life, insights into scripture, the occurrences of a day, and the data gathered through reading, research, and reflection. The journal records dreams, hopes, imaginings. These are the data with which we work.

A journal is also a place of meeting. The hard data of reality meet our dreams and goals. Fusing hard reality with the visions and values of our lives provides a setting for encountering the one who gives ultimate meaning.

The journal provides a place for decision and response. Writing our responses to the revelation of God through scripture, through inspiration, through image, through the events of life, makes the journal a place of accountability. It holds our response to God. And in the future the written commitment holds us accountable.

A journal facilitates integration. It is the matrix in which we connect the truth of today with the larger truth of our life. Not only does it connect with the larger flow of our personal life but with our primary community and, beyond that, with the larger purpose of God.

We will enhance our growth as we use the journal to record the data of our lives brought to our consciousness by the work of the Spirit. The journal provides an arena in which truth is born, decisions are made, meaning is created, and accountability is established for the union of our lives with the larger purpose of God.

Uses of a Journal

The spiritual journal is not a diary. A diary contains occurrences, observations, and descriptions. The diary usually makes no effort to connect external events with an internal meaning and ultimately with the purpose of God. The spiritual journal, by contrast, seeks that end. While the journal collects external data, it does so primarily to discern their inner meaning.

A few suggestions may help. As you begin a journal, write regularly, but don't feel guilty if you miss a day. Experiment with the forms of journal writing as you feel comfortable with them. Work with one discipline until you have exhausted its use for a time. For example, begin by recording your daily prayer experience. Ask what it meant or did not mean to you.

I will describe several ways to use the journal. In each instance I will illustrate with a brief excerpt from my personal journal.

1. I often use the journal when I feel fragmented, when I lack a center. I begin writing by asking, "Where am I in my life?" I begin writing all those things that have been happening to me. I read it over. I look at the events, the feelings, the use of time, my priorities, sin, activities, and the significant persons or occurrences. As I write about these "happenings," I get a "feel" for what is going on with me. This reflection helps to draw my life together.

Here is an entry from August 3.

In gathering up the summer, I must ask myself, "What have I been doing with my life for the last two months?"

June 1—Evaluations and recommendations of my peers. I'm making progress toward tenure and a place on the faculty.

June 10—A week at the beach, interrupted by a trip to Chicago. Got blistered for the last time in my life.

June 17—A week at Lake Junaluska playing golf and bridge and goofing off.

June 24—A week in the office to catch up with registrations for the School of Evangelism.

July 1—Family Life Conference at Montreat.

July 5—Prepared for the School of Evangelism. Four days at the beach.

I've discovered that it is more valuable to have a week's School of Evangelism than a two-day conference on evangelism.

I found this summer that there's not much rest in being constantly on the go. Next summer I want to spend a month in one place doing nothing.

I haven't wanted to write this summer.

2. I use the journal to project myself into scripture. I find it especially helpful to record my meditations on scripture and the meanings that occur to me.

In my meditation on Luke 4:17–19, these were some ideas that came to me:

The Spirit of the Lord is upon me—As I listen to the depths of my being, this witness rings true. The Holy Spirit is upon me. I cannot turn face-to-face with the Spirit. I cannot command the Spirit. But I am aware that my life has been grasped by God. God's grasp is more like a magnet than a vice. God has captured my attention and interest. The Spirit is using me, awakening my imagination, giving me new images, greater confidence, and a sense that the events of my life are working out so that God's will is being done, though perhaps fragmentarily. At long last I think I've learned I cannot compel the Spirit.

In contrast to being in the flow of the Spirit, I have known the days of the eddy. I spent seven years before coming to Columbia Seminary making numerous starts, developing programs, writing, fulfilling speaking engagements that bombed, not sure that I wanted to be a minister, a loss of interest in transcendence, a vague sense of call, frenzied activity to fill the empty spaces in my life.

As I began to listen to my depths, the Spirit spoke. "You will see greater things in the future than you have seen in the past."

3. I use the journal to record my search for guidance. I often ask the question, "What do I most want to do with my life?" I make a list of possible answers. Then I raise the question, "To what extent do these desires manifest or conflict with the Spirit of Jesus Christ?"

On January 6, 1978, I made a list of seventeen things

that I wanted to do during that year. Unless I plan my life, the time slips away and I do not get the things done I intended to do. Here is the list I wrote:

1. Complete the D.Min. degree.
2. Develop a communications program.
3. Study *Alive Now!*
4. Write a new emphasis on stewardship, human survival, and Christian response.
5. Paraphrase Volume IV of the New Testament.
6. A three-day silent retreat.
7. Develop a confirmation resource for distribution to the churches.
8. Compose and write Stewardship II.
9. Revise *You Have a Place.*
10. Develop *The Spirit of the Church* as a program.
11. Work in the area of family life.
12. Write and revise the *Crossbearer* emphasis.
13. Rework creative ideas for summer.
14. Check out completing the Ph.D. degree.
15. Develop a new Christmas program.
16. Pastor a church?
17. Teach a class.

These phrases won't mean a great deal to you. Most of them refer to programs and resources I was developing at the Institute of Church Renewal. Several of these goals are particularly interesting. I did complete the D.Min. degree and in 1978 developed most of the programs that are listed above. But the thought of completing the Ph.D. and pastoring a church was strange to me. I had given up the Ph.D. years before and never intended to complete it. When I finished pastoring a church in Phenix City, Alabama, a decade earlier, I had planned never to pastor again.

Thus, I find it somewhat astounding that my destiny

was intimately tied to finishing the Ph.D. and to having recently pastored a church. When I was called to Columbia Seminary to teach evangelism, the search committee wanted a person who had three basic qualifications: first, that he was coming from the pastorate (I was serving as an interim pastor at the time); second, that he had a Ph.D. degree; and third, that he could develop and produce programs for the local church.

I'm glad that I had a record of my intuitions and dreams of January 6, 1978.

4. I use the journal to free myself from rigid perceptions and commitments. I try to sort out my life and begin listening to God. On March 24, 1981, I made this entry in my journal:

I'm feeling confused, fragmented, spread out. What priority must I have? What order must be given to my life? Here are my plans that are now in motion: weekly classes—five classes with seniors—Evangelism Conference in August—Lay Conference in October—Writing Join the Church—*preparing a course on story evangelism—publishing a newsletter—form an advisory committee—Atlanta Presbytery Council—PATH committee—weekly meetings with churches.*

God, I turn to you deliberately and intentionally for guidance. Let me be aware of your Holy Spirit. What are you saying to me?

[I heard:]

"You must keep yourself open to me, that I can show you my plan for renewing the church.

"It is not in the multiplication of activities, but in the power of my Spirit, that you will give leadership.

"Now you must live in me and let me act through you without being self-conscious. 'Not I, but Christ.' Maybe you have the maturity now to be a servant."

5. I use the journal to record my hunches and intuitions. On December 10, 1978, I recorded these impressions.

I feel my life moving into a new plane, a deeper mean-
ing—maybe. First, I have felt for five months like "a
servant of the Lord in waiting." I've had a return of the
urge to preach, to speak to groups of persons. When I
have done so, I have felt great freedom.

Second, I will be able to resume the Ph.D. studies at
Emory. I believe I will get the dissertation written this
time. It seems to be part of my future.

Third, I enjoy writing, and I still want to write and
communicate my ideas. A glimpse of the future looks
like I'll be writing and distributing my ideas to other
people.

These were hunches and intuitions that came to me three years before I was invited to be a professor of evangelism at Columbia Seminary.

Here is an insight that came to me on May 30, 1982.

Is the clarity and sincerity of my life a prayer to you?
All that I seek to be aware of is already in your infinite
knowledge. Does my search for integrity, my effort to
be open to my gifts, my desire to change my self-im-
age—does this resonate with your will?

It is as if you hold a perfect image of me, of the fully
actualized possibility of my life. And when I come to
terms with me, I am resonating with you. And that
movement is prayer.

It is the prayer of being—the prayer of union. It is
obedience to you and worship and praise. Here is the
point of union between the temporal and the eternal. It

*is one reality. A flip of perspective and I see the divine
in the midst of life. And I experience the thrusts of the
Spirit here, now, enabling my becoming.*

6. I use the journal to record my deepest conscious desires. As I listen to my deepest desires, I think
they often portend the future. They signal the direction
in which my life is moving. For example, as far back as
1981 I was thinking about teaching a course on the
spiritual life. This did not occur for three years. Here is
my journal entry:

*I would like to teach a course on Thomas Merton.
This would give me a chance to explore the contemplative life and to teach ways of spiritual formation to the
students.*

*One great need in our church is to develop a means
of feeding our people. We need to enable persons to
experience the God of grace who comes near to us,
calls us, sets us on his way.*

*Before me I see a vision. A vision of God-centered life.
I will to move with God's Spirit, but I know not how,
when, even if, I will be brought there. The vision which
shapes itself on the edge of my perception consumes
all my natural talent at planning, organizing, promoting,
and motivating. What is left is nothing but God. God
alone, and that is enough.*

*You are calling me! I seem to know it. You're calling
me to be part of what you intend. Let me be open to
you, sensitive to your Holy Spirit.*

*Reveal to me through the normal events of life, the
meetings, the encounters with ministers, chance conversations and unexpected events—reveal to me the
truth, the movement of your Spirit.*

7. I write most of my night dreams in my journal. In early 1984 I recorded this dream.

I dreamed last night that I was on a scavenger hunt. I had jumped in the car and was dashing off to gather all the items on my list when suddenly it occurred to me that I did not even have the list! I had to return to the place of origin to get a list of the things I was seeking.

As I began reflecting on this dream, its meaning seemed so obvious to me. It came at a time when I was hurrying around in my activities with no time for anything. I was eating more, resting less, with my blood pressure going up by the day.

I believe that the dream was revealing to me the internal working of my spirit and sending me a very strong message to stop, slow down, take care of myself, stop acting like a fool who goes hunting for objects without even knowing what they are.

I did stop.

8. I find my journal a place to make confessions. I can say to God on the pages of the journal what I feel most deeply. I pour out my emotions. This enables me to externalize my sin, guilt, and conflict. Sometimes we do not trust another person enough to say all the things that we need to say.

On May 9, 1982, I found myself making this confession.

Dear God, I appreciate the peace of being fifty years old. For ten years I've been at peace with myself, and that is so different from the anxiety and depression of my first forty years. I appreciate it very much. I can't help wondering if I ought to do more with the gift which has been given me.

Do more! It reminds me that I have scheduled myself too heavily. I've no time for myself. No time to recover, to think, to hear new things you might be saying to me.

Hear my confession: neglecting quiet concentrated prayer—compulsive eating—being on the go with back-to-back appointments—not wanting to visit my mother in the nursing home.

I pray for help, for an awareness of choices and the power to decide today.

9. Finally, I use the journal to make lists of persons for whom I'm praying. These are friends, family members, persons with whom I work, persons whom I meet in the course of my work. They ask for prayers, and if I write down their names and their requests, I remember to pray for them.

I am not as ardent an intercessor as I would like to be. I do, however, believe that intercessory prayer is a very important ministry of the church. And keeping lists of those persons and things about which we are praying will make us more disciplined and more steadfast in our prayers.

Values of Keeping a Journal

Perhaps these glimpses into real-life experiences say more than any reflections I can make on them. Nevertheless, here are the ways the journal has been valuable to me. Possibly it may have these values for you also.

The journal offers a way to objectify our feelings and intuitions. It enables us to concretize and externalize them. Recording them in the journal gives a sense of relief, like having been pregnant with an idea or intuition and then being delivered of it. Writing detaches us from our dreams. In a way writing is like telling another person: you make the idea or the sin or the confession external to yourself, and that enables you to be more objective in dealing with the data of your life.

Writing in a journal has an attracting, almost magnetic multiplying effect. In some ways writing draws out our depth more than talking to another person does. Writing is like drawing water from a well. The rope has multiple buckets attached. Each word we write draws another and another; as we continue to pull, the line draws material out of us of which we were totally unaware.

We know more than we are aware of. We are aware of more than we can say. Writing has its own creative power, which enables us to formulate knowledge that we never consciously possessed.

Writing also clarifies our own thoughts. Thoughts that are vague, nebulous, and inexpressible become clearer when we write them down. For example, each time I ask the question, "Where am I in my life?" and write the answer, the data of my present experience become much sharper and clearer to me than before my writing.

Work in the journal invites dialogue. We may begin with the data of our lives, a dream, a vision, a passage of scripture. As we begin asking questions of that data, something within us begins responding. These dialogical experiences engage the material of our lives in a creative encounter that resolves conflict and integrates insights into the fabric of our lives.

***The journal also helps us to discern the trends of
our lives.*** When we read over a journal containing two
or three months' or two or three years' worth of writing,
we can ask some very important questions:

    1. What has had my attention for the last six
months?
    2. What has my energy been focused on?
    3. What themes keep recurring in my life?
    4. Where am I struggling, resisting the presence of
God?
    5. For what am I longing?

These kinds of questions presuppose that the concrete events of our lives reveal the work of the Spirit,
enabling us to discern what the Spirit is doing and
where the Spirit is leading us.

Getting Started with Journal Keeping

First, decide that you want to keep a journal. You may
decide to keep a journal for the next six months and to
use it in conjunction with the various exercises in this
text and in *To Pray God's Will.* Or you may decide to
keep a journal permanently, a much more difficult decision to make and sustain.

Second, secure an appropriate notebook for your
journal entries. My favorite is a bound record book,
which may be obtained at any office supply store or
supermarket. Other teachers recommend a loose-leaf
notebook. A friend of mine keeps his journal on a computer. You may simply choose a plain spiral notebook.
Whatever you select, it should be easy to handle, simple
to store, and private.

Be sure to date each entry in your journal—month,
day, and year. When I began keeping a journal in my
college days, I referenced entries only with a day and

a month. Now I have no idea what year I wrote them. As time goes on, the years begin to blend together, and it's impossible to remember when certain entries were made.

I like to write in longhand. Some persons prefer to type, but my own prejudice is in favor of a felt-tip pen and handwritten notes. For some reason I feel closer to handwritten notes than I do to typed ones. They seem to convey the emotion and feeling of my life more than the impersonal strokes of a typewriter key. Also, when I write by hand, my ideas take firmer shape as they flow onto the page. "The hand is closer to the heart."

As you begin a program of journal writing, sketch an overview of your life. Begin with the marker events, the "chapters" of your life. You may wish to refer to Appendix B for the sequencing of those chapters.

When you begin your structured prayer experiences, reflect each week on what that week has yielded in spiritual growth, in a deeper awareness of God, and in the deepening of your life.

Write your meditations on scripture.

Use the journal for your contemplative writing. As you enter imaginatively into passages of scripture, listen to the the Spirit. Write your reflections.

Reflect on praying the liturgy. What do you discover? What happens to you when you pray the liturgy?

Use the journal in the other ways I have identified. Let yourself be bold in experimenting with new forms of encounter with God. The exercises in Appendix B of this book and in Appendix A of *To Pray God's Will* provide ample suggestions for getting started.

Appendix B

Exercises

Reading about the spiritual journey has little practical value. New ideas are of value only when we reflect on our life with God. One aid to the process of reflection is a personal spiritual journal. (See Appendix A.)

The journal may be any type of record, from a spiral notebook to a computer. The journal contains your insights and spiritual discoveries. It is both personal and private.

These exercises offer guidance in the types of entries to make in your journal. They may also be used with classes or groups.

Exercise 1: How Life Is like a Journey

The following statements describe various aspects of a journey. Using these descriptions, answer each of the questions in a few sentences. These data will provide the substance for your first reflection.

Life is like a journey because . . .

Journeys have points of departure: origins, beginnings. When did your journey begin?

Journeys have movement. What movement do you see in your life?

Journeys have a destination. Where are you going?

Journeys have landmarks that indicate where you are in relation to your destination. Where are you now?

Journeys occur in relationship to time: the past, the now, the future. What time is it on your journey?

Journeys are often made with others: family, friends, spouses. Who are your companions?

Journeys have purpose. Why are you making this journey?

Journeyers keep records: logs or journals or diaries filled with impressions, encounters, and reflections. What record do you have of the journey thus far?

Journeys require preparation. How have you prepared for the journey?

Journeys need directions: maps showing routes and stopovers. What do you depend on to guide you on your journey?

Journeyers engage in taking perspective. How long have you been on this trip? How fast are you traveling? What is your present position? How much farther before you reach your destination?

These parallels make the journey metaphor a good choice for describing the unfolding of our lives, for imaging the spiritual journey. Life is not a static process but a dynamic one, which unfolds with increasing complexity and greater and greater possibilities.

Reflect on the above data. What do they reveal about the journey of your one and only life?

Exercise 2: The Chapters of Your Life

To encounter your life journey more deeply, the following chronological outline with several questions will enable you to resurrect more of your personal history. You may wish to use this exercise after completing the one described in chapter 2 in which you identified the marker events in your life.

Sit quietly, read the question or suggestion, let ideas and memories surface. Make yourself notes and proceed to the next question. Opening yourself to these directives will place you squarely in the flow of your life, from your early years to the place where you are now.

The First Six Years

Very gently go back to your birthplace.

Picture the house, the yard.

Now, enter the house.

Recall the people who are living there.

Go into your favorite room.

Remember the games you played.

What were your joys?

Remember the feelings you had about yourself. About life.

How was the house heated?

Picture the table where you ate and the faces around the table.

Who were the significant persons in this house?

What images of God did you have in this period of your life?

What name would you give to this period?

Think of a symbol, a picture that portrays this period of your life.

Spend several minutes reviewing these suggestions and questions. Let the images, persons, experiences, and events of the past cluster in your mind. Out of your own creativity, name this period and create a symbol for it.

Ages 6 to 12

Recall where you lived, if different from your earlier years.

Recall the freedom and spontaneity of these years.

Who were the significant persons in your life outside the family circle?

What were the significant events that composed this period of your life?

Were there other children in your family?

How did you relate to them?

What were your images of God?

Did you experience feelings of guilt and shame?

How did you handle them?

Do you remember happy times—moments of extreme joy?

What pain do you recall from this era?

What would you name this period of your life?

How would you symbolize it?

Ages 13 to 18

Recall the turbulence of your adolescent years.

What fears do you remember?

How did you relate to the opposite sex?

Recall your first date.

What was the most embarrassing experience of your adolescence?

What were the life-shaping events of your life?

Who were your heroes?

What was Jesus like?
Recall any disappointment or pain.
What conflict did you have with your parents?
What type of spiritual experience did you have?
What was God like to you?
What would you name this period of your life?
What symbol would you use to describe it?

Ages 19 to 30

Recall your first experience of sex.
Remember your first days after leaving school.
What decisions did you make about work?
Did you find a mate? Become a parent?
What did independence mean to you?
What were your first successes and failures as an adult?
What were the goals you established for yourself?
What was intimacy like for you?
How were you committed to Christ in this era of your life?
What was God like for you?
Name this period of your life.
What symbol would you give to this period?
What regrets do you have over the choices you made?
Have you been able to resolve those regrets?

Ages 31 to 40

What was your life dream?
How did you pursue that dream?
With what results?
Is your dream dead today? Or alive?
Has your dream been put aside for another?
Has it been fulfilled?

What is or was the powerful driving force in your life between ages 31 and 40?

What has blocked your fulfillment?

What has opened the way for you to realize it?

What is your role in this period?

What was God like in this period?

How did God relate to your dreams?

What would you name this period?

What symbol would you give to it?

Ages 41 to 50

This period marks a time for maturing and settling into the person you were created to be. It marks the shift from the external world of things to the inner world of spirit.

What resolution have you made of the dream of your life?

What contributions have you made to life?

What have you given that you want to fight for and preserve?

What have you had to say good-bye to in this period of your life?

What was your spiritual experience like in this period?

How does your experience of God compare with other periods of your life?

What name would you give to this period?

What symbol would you use to express it?

The Later Years

What is really important to you in this period of your life?

What have you achieved that you feel proud of?

What do you know now that you wish you had known thirty years ago?

What are some of the things in life you are having to let go of?

How do you feel about saying good-bye to them?

What is God like to you? How would you describe your relationship with God?

What name would you give to this chapter of your life?

What would be an appropriate symbol for describing this chapter?

Examining Your Life Story

Having recalled these experiences and having begun to put into words the meaning of your life, it is important to review your life—to get a feel for it.

Read over the chapter titles of your life. Look at the symbols you have given to your life.

Can you feel the flow of life within you? Can you sense that your life has a movement of its own? The events you have recalled are you. You have been touching the episodes of your life story.

Where is your life now seeking to go? What barriers do you face? What needs to be resolved?

Exercise 3: Reflections on Your Journey

In Exercise 2 I invited you to identify the marker events in your life and to symbolize the substance of each chapter of your life by giving it a name.

In your journal list on the left-hand side of the page the chapters of your life. Leave three or four inches of space between each of your chapter titles.

Go back now and read over the chapters of your life again. Listen for the sound of God. Listen for God, who has created you, has sustained you, and has come to you through the providential happenings of your life. Listen for that Presence.

Remember that God wills to be known to you through the events of your life. God is present in, with, through, and under these events. What has God been saying to you? Through you?

Even now, as you reflect on your own sacred journey, God speaks through your feelings, perceptions, and intuitions. Listen to them.

You are the one and only you. And it is to you and through you that God wills to be revealed. You have never been before, nor shall ever be again. In this unique journey on which you have traveled, God seeks to be known to you in a special way. God seeks to work through you. Listen. Listen for God.

Recall the events that compose the substance of each chapter of your life. Bring them vividly to consciousness. Ask yourself such questions as "Where is God in this chapter of my life? What was God saying to me through these seminal events? To what extent was I aware of God in this period of my life? How was God preparing me in this chapter for a later period of my life?"

Use the space you have created after each chapter to record the perceptions these questions evoke. Don't be afraid to release your creative imagination as you seek to answer these questions.

Suppose that your life is a "word of God" being spoken to the world. In a short paragraph describe what that word may possibly be.

Exercise 4: Helps with Prayer

Make a grid like the one following, recalling your experiences with prayer from your childhood, youth, and adulthood. Developing such an "autobiography" is helpful both for individuals and for discussion in groups.

An Autobiography of Prayer

	childhood	*youth*	*adulthood*
Image of God			
Significant person(s)			
Mode of prayer			
Role of church			
Spiritual experiences			
Meaning of faith			
Greatest resistance to God			

Chapter 4 introduced you to structured prayer. Turn to that structure and read the suggestions. Pause to follow each one. Record the ideas that come to mind as you reflect on each of the movements of prayer.

Continue this practice for a week or two. Writing down your reflections will help you with your consistency. Review the changes that occur over several days.

The two work sheets that follow are useful in teaching a prayer class. The first helps identify common problems; the second helps class members sort out their ideas about prayer. I am indebted to my colleague, Robert H. Ramey, Jr., Professor of Ministry, Columbia Theological Seminary, who created each of these instruments and graciously consented for me to use them.

Reproduce "Problems in Prayer" on one sheet and distribute a copy to each member of the class. Have class members circle those problems that apply to them and then identify the one that is most troublesome. Discussing these problems with the leader or in a small group is often helpful.

Problems in Prayer

Circle the problems that bother you.

1. My mind wanders when I pray.
2. I don't have time to pray.
3. I have doubts about the power of prayer.
4. I pray for myself and my family only.
5. I find it hard to be honest with God about my feelings.
6. I feel that my prayers are too unimportant for God to take any interest in them.
7. I simply don't discipline myself to pray.
8. I find it hard to pray for my enemies.
9. I'm afraid that God will ask me to do something I don't want to do.
10. I find it hard to discover God's will when I pray.
11. I'm too concerned about saying nice words when I pray in public.
12. I have a hard time "feeling the presence of God."
13. I talk too much rather than listen when I pray.
14. My prayer life is hot and cold.
15. I feel like my prayers seldom are heard by God. They bounce off the wall.
16. I wonder why I should tell God what I need, because God already knows me thoroughly.

17. When I get very upset, it's harder for me to pray.

18. I only pray when I'm in trouble.

19. I'm scared to death to pray in public.

20. I find it hard to pray with my spouse or other persons.

When I teach a class on prayer, I copy the following statements on "Thinking About Prayer" but I *omit* the author's name and the source until after the class discussion. When the class has followed the instructions, I engage them in a discussion of those statements which describe their concepts, the ones they question or do not understand, and the ones with which they disagree.

Thinking About Prayer

Read the following statements describing prayer. Circle four statements that best describe your concept of prayer. Place a question mark by the statements you question or don't understand. Place an X by the statements with which you disagree.

1. "Prayer does not change God but changes the one who offers it."—Søren Kierkegaard

2. "Prayer is opening up one's life to God. Prayer opens our lives to God so that his will can be done in and through us, because in prayer we habitually put ourselves into the attitude of willingness to do whatever God wills."—Harry Emerson Fosdick

3. "The primary purpose of prayer . . . is to be with someone. Prayer is the cultivation and expression of a relationship. The primary purpose of prayer is to be with God."—Ted Ferris, Trinity Church, Boston

4. "When we pray for others, certain things hap-

pen that would not otherwise happen. Perhaps they occur as we expect, perhaps not. But when people pray they have a certainty, on the basis of evidence observed by the outward eye as well as the eye of faith, that things are taking place because of their prayer. . . . When you stop praying, coincidences stop."—William Temple[1]

5. In prayer be natural before God. You do not have to act pious before God, or holy, or spiritual. "You are meant to be honest. Do not, therefore, try to hide your true feelings from God."—John Coburn[2]

6. "A Christian fellowship lives and exists by the intercession of its members for one another, or it collapses. I can no longer condemn or hate a brother for whom I pray. . . . Intercession means no more than to bring our brother into the presence of God, to see him under the Cross of Jesus as a . . . sinner in need of grace. . . . To make intercession means to grant our brother the same right that we have received, namely, to stand before Christ and share in his mercy."—Dietrich Bonhoeffer[3]

7. Prayer "demands a relationship in which you allow the other to enter into the very center of your person, allow him to speak there, allow him to touch the sensitive core of your being, and allow him to see so much that you would rather leave in darkness."—Henri Nouwen[4]

8. "We must each take up our own cross, and when we ask something in our prayers, we undertake by implication to do it with all our strength, all our intelligence, and all the enthusiasm we can put into our actions, and with all the courage and energy we have."—Anthony Bloom[5]

9. "The thing that comes first in training for the life of prayer is a healthy relationship with other people.

People do not develop towards God by growing away from fellow humans. The opposite is true."—John Dalrymple[6]

10. "At its deepest level, prayer is not something *we* do, but something which the Holy Spirit does *in* and *through* us. To say we 'ought' to pray is like saying we ought to breathe."—James Fenhagen[7]

11. "Coming to terms with silence is a necessary element in self-knowledge and in prayer. Pascal claimed that 'most of man's troubles come from his not being able to sit quietly in his chamber.'"—Kenneth Leech[8]

12. "Intercession is an affirmation of the interconnectedness of creation, a way of linking up with the life-giving power of God."—James Fenhagen[9]

13. "Prayer is not an activity of the mind, for God is not in the head. It is an activity of the whole person, and God is in the wholeness."—Kenneth Leech[10]

Exercise 5: Liturgy as Prayer

Chapter 5 explored the liturgy as corporate prayer. Take a bulletin from your worship service and write the elements of the liturgy in your journal. Think about each aspect of the liturgy as a form of corporate prayer. After writing your description, picture yourself engaging in this corporate act of prayer with the whole Body of Christ. This visioning will prepare you for worship.

If you don't have a bulletin at hand, use the following liturgy from the Presbyterian *Worshipbook.*

CALL TO WORSHIP
HYMN OF PRAISE
CONFESSION OF SIN

DECLARATION OF PARDON
RESPONSE
PRAYER FOR ILLUMINATION
OLD TESTAMENT LESSON
NEW TESTAMENT LESSON
SERMON
CREED
THE PRAYERS OF THE PEOPLE
THE PEACE
OFFERING
PRAYER OF THANKSGIVING
THE LORD'S PRAYER
HYMN
CHARGE
BENEDICTION

For one month write in your journal your reflections on corporate prayer. What happened to you? How was the worship service different? Did it affect the minister? The sermon? What effect would it have if everyone shared the preparation and corporate prayer experience?

Exercise 6: Writing a Confession

Use the following suggestions and questions as guidelines for writing the confession of your life.

I. Begin with your body. Confess who you are physically.
   1. Describe yourself physically.
   2. Identify the things you like about your body.
   3. What don't you like about your body?
   4. Write your deepest feelings about your body.
   5. Spend time thinking about your physical being.

II. Reflect on your self-image.
1. What is your image of yourself?
2. Do you like yourself?
3. Are you an introverted or extroverted person? How do you feel about your orientation?
4. Are you a thinking or a feeling person?
5. What do you enjoy doing with your time?
6. What are your feelings about yourself?

III. Examine your values.
1. Make a list of things important to you.
2. Name ten things that you desire most in your life. Prioritize them.
3. What gives you the key to the arrangement of your values?
4. Did you freely select these values?
5. Who benefits from the values in your life? You, God, others?

IV. Review your life commitments.
1. Name your lifelong commitments.
2. What are your present but temporary commitments?
3. To what are you committed in life and in death?

V. Reflect on your significant relationships.
1. Who are the ten most significant persons in your life today?
2. Who are the three most important?
3. Describe these relationships.
4. What do you give each of these persons? What do you receive?
5. What is your most difficult relationship? What can you do to correct it?

VI. Consider your vocation.
>   1. Describe what you consider to be God's call-
>   ing in your life.
>   2. What rewards do you receive from your work?
>   3. What are the major problems, if any, with your
>   job?
>   4. How does your vocation glorify God?
>   5. What gifts of yours does your work employ?
>   6. If you could change one thing in your work,
>   what would it be?

VII. Focus on your dreams for the future.
>   1. What is the secret dream of your life?
>   2. Where are you in the process of fulfilling your
>   life's dream?
>   3. What obstacles must you overcome?
>   4. Who can you count on to assist you?
>   5. When your life is over, what would you like it
>   to have meant? To whom?

Notes

Preface

1. Albert Schweitzer, *The Quest of the Historical Jesus* (New York: Macmillan Co., 1968), p. 403.

Chapter 2: The Substance of the Journey

1. Frederick Buechner, *The Sacred Journey* (San Francisco: Harper & Row, 1982), pp. 77–78.

Chapter 4: Prayer and the Spiritual Journey

1. W. E. Sangster, *Teach Me to Pray* (Nashville: Upper Room, 1959).

2. John T. McNeill, ed., *Calvin: Institutes of the Christian Religion,* Vol. XX, Library of Christian Classics (Philadelphia: Westminster Press, 1960), p. 35.

3. Urban T. Holmes, III, *A History of Christian Spirituality* (New York: Seabury Press, 1981), pp. 79–80.

4. Carlo Carretto, *I Sought and I Found* (Maryknoll, N.Y.: Orbis Books, 1984), p. 21.

Chapter 5: Worship and the Spiritual Journey

1. Richard J. Foster, *Celebration of Discipline* (San Francisco: Harper & Row, 1978), pp. 141–142.

Chapter 6: Getting the Journey in Focus

1. Thomas H. Green, S.J., *Opening to God* (Notre Dame, Ind.: Ave Maria Press, 1977), p. 75.

Appendix B: Exercise 4

1. William Temple, quoted by John B. Coburn in *Prayer and Personal Religion* (Philadelphia: Westminster Press, 1957), p. 44.

2. Ibid., p. 17.

3. Dietrich Bonhoeffer, *Life Together* (New York: Harper & Row, 1954), p. 86.

4. Henri Nouwen, quoted in James C. Fenhagen, *More Than Wanderers: Spiritual Disciplines for Christian Ministry* (New York: Seabury Press, 1978), pp. 39–40.

5. Anthony Bloom, *Beginning to Pray* (New York: Paulist Press, 1970), p. 65.

6. John Dalrymple, a spiritual director quoted by Kenneth Leech in *Soul Friend: The Practice of Christian Spirituality* (San Francisco: Harper & Row, 1980), p. 171.

7. Fenhagen, *More Than Wanderers*, p. 29.

8. Leech, *Soul Friend*, p. 179.

9. Fenhagen, *More Than Wanderers*, p. 35.

10. Leech, *Soul Friend*, p. 173.